FOREST LIVES

Number Four

The Thirtieth Anniversary Edition

The Dean Writers' Circle

Edited by Toni Wilde and John Stanley

Published by Blue Funk in association with the Dean Writers' Circle – first published in 2008.

Project Editors – Toni Wilde and John Stanley.

A CIP Catalogue record for this book is available from the British Library

ISBN   978-0-9535473-1-9

Printed and bound by Think Ink Ltd, 11-13 Phillip Road, Ipswich, Suffolk. IP2 8BH

Contents

Editorial

There is a plaque in Gloucester Cathedral commemorating the life of Albert Mansbridge, 1876-1952. He founded the Workers' Educational Association and had he not done so, the Dean Writers' Circle might never have existed and this Anniversary Edition of Forest Leaves would not have been written.

Thirty years ago, a WEA course in Creative Writing was held in Lydney, Gloucestershire. The tutor was Heath Cutler, and although she died some years ago, the seed she sowed has flourished to the present day.

When the course finished in May 1978, a few of Heath's students continued to meet in members' homes, then, in the following August, a proposal to set up a writing circle, to be called The Dean Writers' Circle, was accepted. Two of the original members, John Stanley and 'Another Member' are still active in the group today.

Over the years, the Circle has changed and developed, attracting amateurs and professionals, young writers as well as the more mature. This ensures a wide appeal both to members and their readership.

In making our selection for this book, we have tried to show the range and depth of writing talent that has benefited from the encouragement and criticism available from members of the Circle. We have divided the book into two parts, first a selection of work from current members, secondly, a retrospective selection celebrating the work of writers who for one reason or another are no longer with us

We sincerely hope that you will find the result of our efforts worthwhile and that you will discover much to enjoy in the following pages.

Toni Wilde   **Editors**   *John Stanley*

A NOTE FROM THE CHAIR

Welcome to the Dean Writers' Circle's latest publication of 'Forest Leaves'. Before you peruse and become engrossed in the following pages I would like to take a few moments of your time.

This is the fourth publication in the series and more importantly it is our 'Thirtieth Anniversary Edition'. Because the Dean Writers have met for so many years we decided to honour members past and present. This has indeed been no mean feat and it is as much a tribute to our members as it is to those who compiled this book.

It goes without saying that over time we have lost members, not just because they have passed away but also because they have travelled and settled in pastures new. Because of this there have been many difficulties to overcome; finding and gaining permission from deceased members' families, locating past members and then trawling through the immense amount of work that was sent to us. But, after you have read through to the end of this publication I am sure you will agree that it was worth it.

'Forest Leaves 4' is not only a triumph of assemblage but also a document of the enduring excellence that our members have continued to produce over the years. Several of our members were already published writers before joining us, but it continues to astound me that the quality of all the included pieces is so good.

It only leaves me now to say a huge 'thank you' to everyone who contributed to this anthology, whether professional author or enthusiastic amateur writer. It is my humble opinion that, by showing their passion for writing, all have enriched the work.

I hope that you enjoy reading the book with as much pleasure as we had in writing the pieces.

R.Hayward

THE DEAN WRITERS' CIRCLE

A Personal Account

As a professional writer, disliking the isolation of the occupation, I joined the Dean Writers' Circle, seeking the companionship of like minds in exchange for the encouragement and criticism I was able to give. I found it in abundance ... people I could relate to, who appreciated what help and advice I offered, and who became my friends over the years I was with them.

During an annual general meeting, I was voted in as chairman and took over for a brief spell. Others succeeded me but the format of our meetings remained the same. Then we spread our wings in other directions ... we produced anthologies of our writings under the title of 'Forest Leaves', held open evenings to which the public were invited, participated in events with other writers' circles, organised competitions in poetry and prose, and wrote and staged a couple of pantomimes.

Every meeting was different ... enjoyable, instructive, challenging, inspiring. The writings I listened to and commented on over the years seldom failed to astonish me. Many a time I have been moved to tears or laughed until my sides ached. I have shared the whole gamut of emotions and gained in wisdom, simply by listening to other people's stories or experiences, be they written in poetry or prose. By the simple act of joining the Dean Writers' Circle my life has been enriched...it was a privilege to belong to it.

It's a personal experience, of course. Also personal is my opinion that our human imagination is a precious gift that either we use or lose. I believe we need to exercise, cherish and encourage it all we can in these latter days of mass-produced dross. The Dean Writers' Circle does just that, I think, and I hope it will continue to do so for the next thirty years.

Ten years ago I came to live in the west of Ireland. Leaving the Writers' Circle has been my only regret. I still miss it and always will.

Louise Lawrence

tulip tree

Louise is the author of fifteen books primarily aimed at the teenage market and very much in the Sci-fi and Fantasy genres. She has been published in the UK and in the United States. She has had books adapted for radio. One of her books, *Children of the Dust,* was once a set book for secondary English exams, whilst another *The Power of Stars* was short-listed for the Carnegie Medal.

Part One

Current Members

Maggie Devlin

The Fifty-Pound Slug

Richard patted the soil around the last runner-bean and sat back. Green jewels, crisp and strong, they reached for the sun from their rich bed. He loved them all. He had nurtured them in the greenhouse all spring, beside the courgettes, due out in a few days, and the cabbages, whose blue leaves tinted the far bed beyond the green blades of onions and garlic. He sighed with happiness and reached for the watering can. This was the most beautiful part of gardening.

Tying together the wigwam of beanpoles yesterday, he had frowned at some holes in his young cauliflowers. Cabbage White, probably. He was indulgent towards butterflies. Into every gardener's life must come a few holes. Spotting an early Tortoiseshell fluttering among the candytuft, he smiled. It was all part of the ecology and beauty of the garden. Gardening was mellowness and loving-kindness towards Nature's creatures. There could be few people on Earth who could match a gardener's patience with all living things. He stretched his aching spine and turned back to his greenhouse, where endless pricking-out remained.

That night, it rained heavily. Heads raised and slow bodies were energised. From beneath leaf litter and bark chippings, old planks and ornamental stones, appeared questing, glistening slime, eyes stretching out to the damp night, unseen organs scenting riches on the moist night air. Crispy green feasting was afoot, and so were the gastropods of Gloucestershire.

By early morning, there was naught left but stumps. Richard could only despair at the carnage. The belly-feet, just bellies on feet, had devoured all that lay in their path.

'Greed, it's just sheer greed!' he wept. 'Couldn't they leave me a few? Would it kill them to spare me a mouthful?' He knew then that they were his enemies. Pure evil in slug form. There was no excuse for them.

In their time, molluscs had passed as food, jewellery and even currency, but these were just plain vermin. Richard scoured the gardening books for remedies. They slid over chopped-up hair scattered around the seedlings. Garlic companion-planting was delicious. Jalapeno pepper ? They ate it in big bites.

He haunted the garden centre seeking the final solution. Plastic collars, lime, pine bark, copper bands guaranteed to deliver a shock – for only £5 a foot. He met others, scouring the shelves in mounting desperation. It was the wettest summer in living memory, and slugs were poised to take over the world, but slug pellets were more dangerous than nuclear waste, according to the health warnings. He sprinkled organic slug killer around the crops. It didn't work. He found the container next day. They had eaten the label off it. They loved paper. They ate anything. They came under the kitchen door and ate the cat's food. Cannibalistic, too. After a frenzied slug-stamping session by his less squeamish small daughters, he found several black slugs dining on the remains.

When they ate Chapter Ten of the Pocket Encyclopaedia of Organic Gardening, Richard's heart hardened. The girls were right. All-out warfare was the only way. He didn't like killing things, but for slugs he'd make an exception. When his marigold buds were eaten off without shame or pity, leaving a veritable M1 of slug-slime, he left no stone unturned, but found nothing. Maybe it had a larger range, or was a soil-dweller. He just didn't know enough about them. From that day on, Richard studied his enemy.

There were surprises, like the tiny slug found abseiling from a watering can on a thread of slime, towards a freshly-picked lettuce. One night, patrolling the garden with a torch, he saw an elongated shape on the fence at the bottom of the garden. The moon was rising full over the river. Rearing up like a cobra the slug began to weave slowly and gracefully in the moonlight, always with its eye-stalks stretched towards the light.

Worshipping the moon? For a dreadful moment, Richard caught himself seeing beauty in a slug. He shook his head and went back inside, his mission forgotten.

The day he burned the jam bucket, a horrible smell of burnt sugar announced his mistake. What a mess. Welded on, that was. He'd probably need a new pan for next year. He dumped the problem outside the back door until he could deal with it.

Two days later, glancing inside the pan, he saw a silver gleam. Not a speck remained. Richard picked it up for a closer look, and saw the slug trails leading away. Shrugging, he took it inside to scald with boiling water. Richard didn't realise it, but he'd actually found a practical use for slugs.

Richard's eyes widened as he approached the garden-centre checkout. He was seeing slugs. Pink, three-foot tall, in papier-mache.

'We're having a festival of slugs.' explained the assistant. 'With demonstrations of slug repellent, races, poems and a competition to find the biggest slug. The weigh-in's at two o'clock on Saturday. It's just a bit of fun.' He grinned as he handed Richard an entry form.

That evening, Richard penetrated the labyrinth of sticks behind the compost-heap and found his monster. The biggest slug of all time. A gastropod the size of the Ritz, nearly spherical, glistening brown. He poked it out of the leaf mould, smiling grimly. As it rolled onto the path he raised his boot … and lowered it again. He had plans for this beast.

The Festival of Slugs was a great success. The slug-shaped cakes were a bit disgusting, but the children loved them. Even Richard was surprised at the depth of bitter emotion expressed by the Slug Poetry Recital. A black slug on a well-watered path proved the speediest, a saucer of Kitekat the winning post. Richard commiserated with his colleagues.

'I built slug pubs. Drowned every living thing. Just gave the slugs an appetite. My lettuces were the equivalent of an Indian Takeaway after ten pints. Bastards.'

'Eight new courgette plants. Eight of them! Scoffed the lot. God it makes you despair.'

At the Weigh-in, Richard's slug dwarfed the other competitors, dropped curled-up onto the electronic scale.

'26, 27…28.35 grams. We have a winner!'

One whole ounce of slug. Richard felt proud. Then the manager came towards him with a smile and a cheque for fifty pounds. Richard had never thought to ask what the prize was. Just a bit of fun, after all.

Back home that evening, Richard brooded over the sandwich-box containing his prize-winner. He had kept it damp and fed it bits of lettuce to sustain it. Almost like his daughters' pet hamsters. His prime directive that summer was to kill slugs. But he couldn't kill this slug. It had just won him fifty pounds. He was *grateful* to it.

His heart warred within him. He would have to squash the bastard or it would demolish his dahlias, crucify his chrysanthemums, massacre his marrows. He stared at it, seeing orange frills around the edges of its foot, the humped mantle and pneumostome. There was a sea of minute white dots on its body. Parasites? Slug-bugs? He watched the horrid little things at play on the slug's surface. Slugs have pests, too. Nobody's immune.

His mind was made up. Climbing over the fence into the long grass, he deposited the box and waited. His enemy glided majestically into the dewy grass with the tiniest of rustles.

Yes, gardening was mellowness and loving-kindness towards Nature's creatures. Richard stretched out on his blanket contentedly in the sun.

Into every gardener's life must come a few holes.

Storm in a paint pot

Sophie was upset. This was by no means an unusual state of affairs in the Marks household. Sophie was frequently upset. Maybe she had put on a pound in weight. Or lost a pound in weight - either was disastrous. Had one of her boyfriends dared to accuse her of wearing lavender – a colour long-hated for its association with a particularly large elderly aunt, whose floral-scented demeanour at dinner had all the grace and dignity of a Gloucester Old Spot, or perhaps it was raining when she had specified fine weather for the day. Could it be because the housekeeper had 'tutted' when told to send back Sophie's breakfast order for the fourth time because the coffee was Kenyan instead of Brazilian, there weren't enough hazelnuts in her muesli, the freshly-squeezed orange juice had bits of orange in it?

Or was it simply her father's continued, baffling refusal to move the entire family to an Italian villa so that Sophie could realise a long-cherished ambition – to hear her name pronounced the Italian, and romantic way – Sophia Marconi was far, far sexier than plain old Sophie Marks. Honestly! How selfish could the man be?

Sophie 'Groucho' Marks as she was known to the household staff, had many grievances against her father. For instance, she only had one television in her private suite of rooms – sitting room, bedroom and en-suite bathroom with Jacuzzi. She actually had to decide whether to watch TV in her bedroom OR her sitting room – not both! In vain her father had pointed out that the giant Nicam FST in her sitting room would never fit into the bedroom, so that to watch TV in the bedroom she would have to make do with her old colour portable which she had had since she was FIVE years old! How mean was that? She had immediately thrown the despised little TV out of the window into the swimming pool, and her father, in a rare outbreak of parental discipline, had decreed that she was not to have another. It had taken Bob Jones, the odd-job man, many hours of overtime to drain and clean out the pool to remove all the fragments of glass and circuit boards.

Bob had a great variety of duties – cleaning, repairs, chauffering the family about town, car maintenance and dog-fancying as required. He was often called in for more abstruse matters, however, such as marital advice, financial projection and interior decorating. This hapless seneschal had been with the family since he was sixteen and had watched Miss Sophie grow up – inasmuch as she had achieved maturation so far. Today was going to be a trial, he could see. Sophie was refurbishing her apartment in the manner to which she had become accustomed. 'This is a total nightmare! I can't decide what to have! Melanie Naysmith has her bedroom done in Evening Glory with Hint of Wheat accessories … everything done in rag-rolling, by hand, of course, that's the thing now, or hand-marbling with a sponge, I don't know how she had the patience to keep on at the decorators day after day – and it took them a week!

Sophie strode about the room in her Marilyn Monroe headscarf (retro) and Pegasus sunglasses (post-Ironic, and top of the range).

'I think I'll have a pensive colour in here. All these colours are too loving.' she declared. Sophie's mother exchanged quizzical glances with Bob. What was this claptrap?

'Perhaps I'll have the whole room done in blowpipe-style.' Sophie mused, floating artistically around the echoing bedroom.

Mrs Marks darted an alarmed glance at Bob, she thinking of overtime payments, he dreading the loss of his precious weekend to a spoilt girl's vanity. A bit of painting was one thing, but did she want to recreate Versailles? Bad taste and all?

'No … I think solid colours are right for this space,' Sophie decided at length.

Relieved grins were exchanged. Sophie's tastes, like her

moods were notoriously unstable. Her moods trampolined on an hourly basis.

'What colour though … I want a sort of dusk in the Highlands, with a hint of dim purple hills, with just a touch of midsummer heather coming through … Bob!'

'Yes?'

'I want to go to the paint shop to choose my colour!'

'I'll get the car out' he said resignedly. It was four-fifteen on a Friday afternoon. The nearest DIY store was open 'til eight, though. He knew what that meant.

Two hours later, Sophie's mood was a gathering storm.

'They haven't got MY colour! I hate all these colours! They're not good enough! I'm a posh girl! I can't use these!' she raged, to the opened-mouthed amazement of other shoppers.

'Well, if you can't find a colour to suit you, you can always get one mixed,' suggested the assistant wearily. Only one more hour 'til closing time. Opening time was long past.

'That's perfect!' Sophie gushed. 'I'll have my colour tailor-made! I want a bit of the Evening Dusk and a smidgen of Highland Triumph and …'

'Oh, we can't do it here, today,' said the assistant hastily.

'Why not ?' demanded Sophie.

'Machine's out of order, until we can call the contractors.'

'Oh my God! What kind of rubbish service is that?' Sophie fumed.

'Um. If you come back on Sunday we can do it for you,' offered the assistant.

'Two days … ooh … all right then, I'll do that,' she agreed at last.

Bob could actually see his beautiful, beautiful weekend- what was left of it – floating away from him on little wings.

Sunday afternoon saw them standing expectantly in front of the paint-mixing machine. Sophie held a silk scarf.

'I want this matched exactly,' she declared.

Six attempts later, the required shade, the Holy Grail of paint colours, emerged amid riotous joy in Bob's heart. Trumpets sounded and his hammock and cold beer beckoned in a haze of golden light. He could go home! It was all over!

Three hours later, he corrected his ecstatic statement. It was all over bar the shouting.

'This is horrible! I specifically told that MORON that I wanted Evening Dusk, Highland Triumph and Purple Mist – wasn't he listening! This colour is too loving! It's not pensive! It was supposed to be pensive!!'

Paintspattered and bewildered, Bob surveyed the immaculately-emulsioned walls. It looked like lilac to him.

'It's got to be done again! Honestly I can't live in this room!'

Bob was close to tears.

'You've got to go back, and get some more paint and do it again!'

Two hours later, Bob surveyed the fruits of his trashed weekend.

'Now, that's pensive ... oooh I love it! It's so faux-Victorian – but NOT Victorian! Victorian would be horrible! The Victorians would have done it in lilac. That's all they knew. Lilac! As if! Only old bags use lilac!' Sophie was finally happy in her tonally-adjusted world.

Bob was relieved. All he had to do now was dump the paint cans in the bin and lean exhaustedly against the tiled walls of the shower long enough to get clean, before slumping into his comfy chair in front of the Antiques Roadshow.

Mrs Marks entered the room.

'Oh love! You chose a nice lilac after all instead of all those miserable colours you were looking at! Isn't it nice!' she said, happily.

'Mother! For God's sake! This isn't lilac! Lilac is post-post retro, which makes it passe. This is completely different.'

'Oh, I see, dear,' replied Sophie's mother hastily. 'My mistake. Well, at least you're happy with it.' Sophie's beaming face confirmed this.

Bob staggered out to the dustbin, with an armful of empty paint cans. He lifted the lid of the plastic skip and hurled the paint buckets in.

'B&Q Basics LAVENDER,' they read.

cedar

Maggie is an ex-librarian assistant and road protester currently living in Bream. She is also a part-time conservationist and green activist. She is currently working on a novel about the life of squatters in Bristol. All the slug details are entirely true, and the Festival of Slugs really happened one wet summer.

Maria Edey

- It's Only Rumours
  Chapter One
  - The Hanging   page 17

It's Only Rumours

Chapter 1 The Hanging

September 1685

There was not a sound to be heard that Autumn morning in the village of Stogursey. Tom Hurst and Will Jeffries made their way slowly up towards Tower Hill. Tom looked into the windows of the cottages as he walked by. Not a soul about, how strange, there were usually one or two villagers with candles lit in their windows ready for the day's work. Too bloody frightened to face me. Guilt. Well, they will have ta face me later t'is marning.

They arrived at the top of Tower Hill. 'Planks all 'ere then Tom,' said Will.

'Aye, delivered yesterday marning. Better get on with it.'

The men began laying out the wooden boards to form a box. Rain started to fall lightly. The air around seemed somehow more dense than usual, the sky black, black as coal. Suits the day I suppose, thought Tom. He carried on doing his job.

Bang, bang, he knocked each nail into the hardened wood; at least there was noise. This was a job he didn't want to do. He stood up, wiped the rain from his brow, calling softly to his mate, 'Are ye there Will?'

'Aye Tom, I be 'ere'

'Can ye give me an 'and Will? I just want to finish this piece off afore it gets light.'

'When is it Tom, when these poor souls are to be 'ung?'

'Midday Will. Colonel Kirke 'as to come from Taunton. 'E don't like to miss an 'anging.'

'They didn't stand a chance – Hugh nor John.'

'Kirke and Trelawney and their soldiers, they say, raped, pillaged and bullied the families of the rebels. Me and Evelyn 'id

17

Hugh's wife and young 'uns under potatoes; thought that would be the last place they'd look; dunno how John's wife faired.'

'Not so good by all accounts, but she's a strong lass,' sighed Will.

'There's no 'ope now, not for either one.' Tom wiped a tear away; he was a man but he was not afraid to shed a tear.

'I grew up with Hugh, fine man, honest and trustworthy. He only fought for Monmouth because he believed in freedom. He believed in the Church of England. Not t'other thing. No good going on about it now, too late.'

Tom took up the mallet and started banging more nails in. ''Tis finished. 'Elp us, will ya?'

Tom pushed, Will pulled, until the planks were lying across the wooden platform.

''Ere Will, we 'ave to 'ave the rope 'anging o'er those trap doors steady, slightly to the right, now to make 'e sturdy.' Tom started to finish off. He banged harder, he was angry, this was the only way he could let it go. If he had argued with anyone in authority he would be joining his friend Hugh by now. And what good would that do? Someone had to look out for Hugh's Missus and the young 'uns. Tom's good wife Evelyn had said they would take care of Kate and little Hugh and of course Baby Alice.

'We be dun, Tom. Let's get 'ome and 'ave a bite to eat, we got a long day ahead of uz.'

'Aye, Will, the wuz day of our lives. Two young 'uns will be without their Father, two wives without their men. What will become of them, what will become of them?'

They went back down Tower Hill towards Fore Street, then turning into Castle Street, bade their farewells.

'Who was it Tom, who betrayed Hugh an' John?'

'Quiet Will; best you never know or ya could be the next one 'anging. Keep yourself to yourself. Look after your wife.'

'Till midday, Tom.'

With a wave of his hand Tom carried on down Castle Street

towards his home. He opened the door and walked into the parlour, hung his hat upon the hook. It slipped forwards and water ran onto the flagstones. Evelyn looked up from the stove. She would usually curse her husband for getting the floor wet. Not today. It didn't matter quite so much any more. Neither of them spoke. Eve put the bread on the table, Tom ate silently.

It was drawing closer to midday. The rain was falling faster, heavier. Not much light came through the clouds this Autumn day. Tom sat silently at the kitchen table; he hadn't moved all morning. Tears rolled down his rough, lined face. He was only thirty years old, but already he looked like an old man. The hard life he lived was taking its toll.

'Better get a move on, Tom, it's nearly time.' said Evelyn quietly.

He didn't move. 'Not sure I can do it, Eve.'

'Think of Kate, the young 'uns, they need ya.'

Tom rose from the table, picked up his hat, and without a word went out to the barn to harness his horse to the cart. 'Whoa boy, steady, let me slip this o'er ya 'ead.'

Dong, Dong, Dong, the church bells were tolling, calling the villagers to the hanging. A heavy, sober Dong over and over again. They got on his nerves. 'FOR GOD'S SAKE QUIET DOWN,' he shouted.

'Ya ready Tom?' asks Will coming up behind him.

'Bloody hell, Will, what? Oh aye, I be ready. Grab the reins, let's go.'

They walked slowly towards the pound, where Hugh and John had been kept for ten days, with straw laid down on the stone floor for their bed. Tom had visited Hugh only once – that was all he was allowed. Hugh was in a pitiful state. There was excrement in one corner of the room, their urine ran over the floor. They just had bread and water in the morning. The men could barely stand. It broke Tom's heart to see them. The pound was in Castle Street so Tom and Will did not have far to go. They stopped outside the

19

wooden gates and knocked to be let in.

'Who's there?' asked the guard.

'It is I, Tom Hurst and Will Jeffries. We have come to take the men to the gallows.'

The gates were pulled open by one of the villagers, Walter Bitford – his brother had got off with just a fine. 'Sad day Tom' said Walter.

'Ay 'tis Walter. This be a job that I dunt want to do, but I will do me best for Hugh.'

Walter unlocked the cell door. Hugh walked towards the door with his head held high; he wasn't going to break down now. John was more bent over. Both men were now near just bones. John Herring stumbled. The shackles rattled together they were very heavy – it was hard to walk.

''Ere John take me arm,' said Hugh. 'We'll do this together.'

Tom and Will watched as the two men approached. Tom wanted to put his arm around his friend who he had known since a bairn. But he knew that would not be the best thing to do. Hugh smiled at Tom reassuringly. Hugh and John climbed up into the cart unaided.

The horse moved off with Tom's command, very slowly to the end of Castle Street, stopping to turn into Fore Street. Standing quietly on the corner of Fore Street, the rain running down their thin bodies, were Hugh and John's wives, Kate and Helen. Kate was holding baby Alice close to her, trying to keep the mite dry. Little Hugh was standing by his mother's side.

Hugh looked over to his wife, puckered his lips as if to kiss. Helen was all alone; they had never had the chance to have any bairns. John smiled and mouthed, 'Sorry.'

Tears ran down her cheeks; she answered, 'I love you.'

'Click, click.' Tom moved the horses on. Kate and Helen fell in behind. They walked slowly up towards Tower Hill, heads bowed. They passed shops and cottages in the main street. Once again not a soul about. The villagers had gone ahead, some wanting to get the best view of the hangings. Some of course, stayed in their homes, weeping and praying for their men, two local lads from Stogursey.

They were now near the gallows. The crowd had gathered. Kirke and Trelawny had the only seats which were placed in front of the crowds. They wanted to make sure the job was done right.

Tom drew the horse and cart to a standstill. 'Whoa boy.' He tied the horse to a tree and walked towards Hugh and John. Will was already down and helping the men. The men refused the offer and climbed down from the cart on their own. With heads held high they walked towards the gallows, their wives not far behind silently sobbing.

John walked slowly towards the gallows. Little Hugh looked nervously round; he knew his Father was about to die. Tom noticed that the rain had stopped. Now when did that happen, he wondered; he had not noticed. The sun had started to break through. He smiled – perhaps there is a God after all, and he is looking after Hugh and his mate John.

Kirke was getting impatient. 'Hurry yourselves, I have not got all day!' He yelled loudly, 'I have to be in Bridgewater later today; three more hangings before night draws in.' The men climbed up onto the wooden frame. The crowd was silent, the chattering stopped.

Some of the women had been sobbing, but now seemed to be holding their breath, waiting for the next thing to happen. The Hangman put the noose first round John Herring's neck. Helen called out 'John, we will meet again.' John smiled, a tear ran down his cheek for the first time.

CRACK, THUD, the trap door opened. His body twisted side to side. Then stillness. 'NEXT!' shouted Kirke. Hugh stood tall and straight. He looked towards Kate; she hugged the bairns close to her; little Hugh started to cry. 'Hush little Hugh,' called his father, 'I be only going to 'eaven, take care of yor mam.' With that, the door of the gallows opened. Kate screamed. Tom shouted 'NO!'

The crowd started to break up to make their way home. Tom walked over to his horse. Will ran behind and caught up with Tom. 'Tom don't say a word, but look over there towards Kirke.'

Tom looked. He could see some of the villagers milling around Kirke. Money was changing hands. The villagers passed quickly by; the same people that had denied it was them when questioned. ''Tis only a rumour,' said Richard, 'let me buy ya a drink round at the Swan.' Tom knew who were the ones that betrayed his friend Hugh Ashley, and John Herring.

Richard walked past Tom quickly, his head down, followed by two other men, Andrew Watson and Mervyn Bitstock.

'May you go to Hell, Richard Higgins!' shouted Tom. "MAY YOU ALL GO TO HELL!"

ash

Maria has been writing for over ten years. She writes comedy, drama, humanity scripts and prose for adults and children. Maria was born in the Forest of Dean, has lived overseas and in different parts of the United Kingdom. She has now returned to writing and hopes to have something published, or one of her scripts performed in the theatre in the near future.

22

Betty Gentles

OVERDRIVE

My driving instructor was a laid back sort of chap, so laid back in fact that he practically balanced on the nape of his neck in the passenger seat. The ravaging wolves gnawing at my insides began to look pretty silly in the face of this much confidence and soon dwindled to a butterfly, a half-hearted creature, a mere tickle.

A rapport grew between this man and me that had no need for words. Like John Wayne he'd looked into the jaws of death so often he'd grown philosophical and only emitted the odd 'Yup' or 'Nope' when my questions grew frantic.

He had a scale of expressive grunts from one to ten. As time passed his staccato comments rose and hovered round the eight to nine mark. I knew I was almost ready for the big time when he gave up grunting and snored throughout the entire lesson.

He talked me into applying for my test, beating down my panic-stricken objections with the soothing assurance that the waiting list was enormous. By return of post a letter arrived, giving me a date three days hence. My friendly little butterfly turned and savaged me.

'Three days!' I wailed.

'Yup!'

'Am I good enough?'

'Yup!'

'Wouldn't it be better to wait? Another month perhaps?'

'Nope!'

I spent every spare minute practising and practising. My three point turn was a dream of perfect execution, my reversing so accurate I could have parked on a postage stamp. I was ready!

I woke up on the morning of the test with the father and mother of all colds. Little men with hammers beat my brain, my nose leaked, my eyes would hardly open.

'I'll have to cancel!' I husked to my ghastly reflection in the mirror. But would they give me another date? Would my driving ever reach this pitch of perfection again?

I swallowed aspirin. Miraculously my eyes opened and my nose stopped running. The little men backed off to a reasonable distance. I could still do it!

Two hours and six more aspirins later I was in the car on my way to the Test Centre. My butterfly was dead, or at least unconscious from aspirin poisoning.

John Wayne and I grunted round the designated course one more time. Though I say it myself, I was fantastic – couldn't put a tyre wrong.

We arrived and parked in the yard of the Test Centre. This was IT – THE BIG MOMENT.

The Examiner was a long time coming. I took a couple more aspirins for luck and crouched in the car, trying vainly to remember the Highway Code.

Nervous perspiration stuck my hands to the wheel. My butterfly gave a reviving kick or two, and suddenly I remembered the little pill that lurked in my purse. A friend had pressed a tablet upon me, assuring me that this pill would remove my jitters at a stroke. I blew the fluff from it and sent it down to join the aspirins. I had never taken a tranquiliser before and I have never taken one since.

When the Examiner appeared, I greeted him with a benevolent smile and surprised myself by leaping from the car to open the passenger door. It surprised him too I could see. His rather sad eyebrows rose just a fraction, especially when I insisted on tucking him in and adjusting his seat belt.

Poor little man, I thought. Nobody loves you. Spending your days beside sweating, terrified people who've never driven as badly in their lives. I was going to change all that.

Chattering brightly, I drove into the stream of traffic. Our town has a bit of everything, a large complicated roundabout, an ancient hump-backed bridge, so narrow it only takes one car at a time, a short stretch of dual carriageway, and an astonishing collection of kamikaze children and dogs. They were out in force that day, leaping at me from all angles, but I kept my cool.

'Do you hire all these people?' I asked innocently. A bright little light had begun shining steadily inside my skull. Nonchalantly I jousted with juggernauts and skirmished with Scammels. Unexpectedly my brain went into overdrive. I bubbled with exhilaration.

When a police car joined us for the second time at the traffic lights, I felt the need to make a friendly gesture.

'Yoo Hoo boys!' I cried and gave them a wave. They grinned at my Examiner, who grinned back. It was so lovely, what nice lads!

'Got a right one there.' Somebody said.

I was directed to a quiet street and asked to do an emergency stop on a hill. No bother! This gave me the chance to do a hill start. Dead easy! When we came to a flat stretch of road, he asked for the three point turn. Pathetically simple! I showed him how simple it was by doing it all over again in reverse. He looked surprised.

'What did you do that for? I wanted you facing in the other direction."

'Right' I said, 'but let's do it the hard way.' At the speed of light, my hands and feet a blur of synchronised movement I did an eight-point turn, and drew up with a flourish. My Examiner looked a little flushed.

'Wasn't that fun?' I cried. I could see he was deeply impressed. He was having some difficulty getting the right words out. He pointed to the rear window.

'I want you to reverse round that corner.'

I groaned. How insultingly simple. Why didn't he ask for something difficult? I'd show him!

Carefully I reversed the car up over the edge of the kerb on to the pavement, and keeping the white fence on my left and the kerb on my right, whizzed with breathtaking accuracy round the corner, straight between a lamp standard and a well-clipped hedge.

I stopped and looked proudly at my Examiner who happened to have his mouth open and his eyes shut.

'How about that?' I beamed.

I don't remember much about driving back, though I do recall crying 'Geronimo!' as we sped down the steep hill where I'd done my emergency stop.

I wonder now why he didn't take over the controls. If ever a driver was tranquillised into a state of stupid arrogance I was, but he was still beside me, giggling weakly, when we parked at the Centre.

'Hurrumph!' he said, pulling himself officially together. Tears were streaming from his eyes.

'I'm very sorry' he gasped. 'But I can't pass you,' I gave the jolly good fellow a slap on the back.

'Quite right' I said. 'You'd be a fool if you did!'

I sang joyfully all the way home. My driving instructor drove and rather tersely refused to join in the choruses.

I sometimes wake in the night and relive the sight of that Examiner hauling himself up the iron staircase outside the Test Centre, his free hand pressed in agony to his stomach.

I can never go back there – never! – at least not until that man retires. But they probably retire early. It must be a very wearing job.

SAD SOCK SAGA

They come in pairs, at birth they're twins,
Caress your ankles, smooth your shins;
Entwined together snugly lie
Within the drawer when they're put by.
But tell me why – Achee, Achone,
Why do they aim to be alone?

I put six pairs in my machine,
Some brown, some grey, some Lovat Green.
But when the dryer comes to rest
There's six all different in a vest.
Divorced, their partners cling ecstatic
To other garments drunk with static.

The rot sets in – first one then t'other
Are solitary in the drawer
And though I search with mounting fervour,
Their missing friends are gone forever.
Oh hear their woolly-minded talk
My partner ran off with a frock.

One night my husband had a shock,
He found my bag of lonely socks.
He, to my explanation hearkened
'Til jealousy his features darkened.
The truth I'll have – tell me no other!
Who is this damned one-legged lover?

THE HEAD START

George was the landlord of the Pea and Whistle, and Sybil had worked there for six weeks, three days, and, he looked at the bar clock, two hours and ten minutes. Oh, he had it bad, had George. He could hardly take his eyes off her long enough to serve customers and old Jimmie Wilson had to ask for his bitter three times before he heard him above the musical chimes that rang every time Sybil squeezed past him in the narrow space behind the bar.

George was so engrossed with the sheer poetry of her white arms pulling a pint that he hardly noticed Partington whispering in her ear. Partington was a commercial traveller and a resident at the Pea and Whistle.

'Oh, you are a one, Mr. Partington!' she giggled, tossing her golden head. Mr. Partington pushed his sleek head closer and whispered again.

'Well, alright Bertie – next Monday then.'

George thrust his clenched fists into his trouser pockets and his scowl was so black, Bertie took an involuntary step back.

'There's a customer been waiting in the Lounge Bar ten minutes, Sybil,' he said harshly. Sybil looked very surprised at the tone, but went past him obediently. George ignored the frantic pleas from Jamie Wilson and his empty pint-pot, and followed her smartly. The Lounge Bar was empty as he knew very well.

'What was that Partington saying to you?'

'Saying to me? Why, nothing much.'

'Did you say you'd meet him next Monday?' In his agitation he put his great hand on her shoulder and shook her slightly.

'Stop pushing me around, George McDonald. I can do what I like on my day off. Besides I rather like him. He behaves like a gentleman – and he's got gorgeous hair! All thick and shiny!' This last dig was pure mischief, for George's rusty coloured thatch was getting pretty thin on top. George looked into her tantalising blue eyes, and he could feel the wrath draining out of him.

'Sybil, you know I'm mad about you!'

'Yes, George, but you don't do anything about it. A girl likes to be taken out now and then!' and she turned and flounced back to the bar where the plaintive cries for refreshment had become a chorus.

George sat in his cosy little parlour that night, pondering bitterly over his problem. In the drawer of his desk were two tickets for the big Brewers Dance to be held next Monday, the very night Partington was taking Sybil out. Blast his stupid hide for keeping it such a secret, but then he hadn't been sure until today that he could get someone to cover the bar on Monday. He blasted himself and Partington, and his black hair. Take away his hair, and what was he – nothing but a silly little man with a smart line of patter, not fit even to touch the hem of Sybil's skirt. The girl didn't realise – she must be protected.

It was then that the worst idea he had ever had entered George's head. He recoiled from it in horror, but it crept in again. It was too diabolical, even for Partington – besides it was bound to have flaws. He examined the idea very carefully. It was horrible – but if it worked – oh my sainted aunt if it worked ... A great chuckle escaped him. He'd be taking Sybil to the dance after all.

Early next morning he left the pub and took a bus to the outskirts of town. He didn't ask directions. Well, he might be remembered afterwards, so it took quite a bit of searching before he found the little chemist tucked away in a back street, and he was in, asking for the stuff.

Back at the Pea and Whistle, he slipped silently through the front door, and who should be coming out of the dining room but Partington himself.

'Cor, you're out bright and early old man!' He shrugged himself into his dark overcoat, and ran a hand over his sleek hair. George watched him with loathing while the young man eyed himself in the mirror. 'Got to look smart you know, old man – the girls love it.'

He leaned over and gave George a confiding dig in the ribs. 'That's a bit of alright you've got behind the bar, eh? I can hardly wait till Monday.' He was whistling as he swaggered out of the door and George's resolve, that had weakened slightly, hardened once more into forged steel. He was going to enjoy wiping out Mr. Partington.

He glanced at his watch. It should be a good half hour before Mrs Winterbottom got round to doing the bedrooms, if she was doing things in her usual order. Mrs Winterbottom obligingly pinpointed her position by bursting into song in the Lounge Bar. Now was the time. On soundless feet he crept up the carpeted stairs and let himself silently into Partington's room with his pass key. Back against the door, he let his gaze travel round the untidy room until it finally came to rest on the cluttered dressing table. Blimey! The little twerp had more toilet preparations than a teenage girl. There was shaving cream, talcum powder, after-shave lotion, tweezers, eau de cologne, deodorant, and a huge jar of hair cream. George eyed the hair cream anxiously. If it were full, he'd have to make another trip.

His hands shook a little as he unscrewed the top and peered inside. Half empty – Good! After a few rather messy moments, he had transferred the hair cream to the plastic bag he had brought on purpose, and began scooping the cream he had just bought into the hair cream jar, until it was just the right level. This was a lot more trouble than he expected. He got it all over his hands, and even a spot or two on his overcoat, but at last the job was done and the hair cream jar replaced exactly where he had found it. He took a large clean handkerchief from his pocket and wiped the jar clear of fingerprints, then using the handkerchief as a shield, turned the handle of the door and sped noiselessly downstairs and into his parlour.

He was sweating furiously and aching for a drink, but

31

checked himself before reaching for his private supply. He must wash his hands. Into a welter of hot soapy water he plunged the hairy guilty objects, and scrubbed and rubbed like demented Lady Macbeth. At length they were pink and smooth, and he reached thankfully for the whisky. SMOOTH! The word registered with a ghastly jolt, and he gazed at his own hands without recognition. The great hairy fists that had been his as long as he could remember were now as smooth and hairless as any woman's. Ye Gods! He sat stunned. Talk about being caught red-handed! Everybody would notice, and everybody would realise that he was the one that had replaced Partington's hair cream with hair removing cream.

There was only one thing to be done. He would have to take the stuff out and put the original cream back in the jar. But he was too late. Even as he opened the door, Mrs Winterbottom started creaking up the stairs, complete with Hoover. He was still gazing worryingly up the stairs when a tap on his shoulder made him twitch like a skittish horse.

'My, aren't we nervous today' said Bert Partington, and gave him a reassuring thump. 'Turned out a miserable day, so I thought I'd come back and spend the day catching up on my books. See you!' He sped up to his room. George tottered back into his parlour and reached once more for the whisky.

By opening time, due to desperation or whisky, or both, George had come up with another brainwave, and both his hands and Sybil's were encased in white cotton gloves, left over from his waiter days. 'Gives the place a bit of class,' Sybil had agreed with a giggle, but though George's white-gloved hands served drinks with their usual efficiency, his anxious eyes hardly left the swing doors.

As it happened, he didn't see Partington's entrance. He was in the Lounge Bar pouring a customer's drink, when he heard the loud shout of laughter that could only mean one thing. He dashed back to the Public Bar and looked. It was Partington all right, hardly recognisable, with a round shining pink dome where his dark hair had been. Everybody was laughing and cheering and offering him drinks. Cor, he did look funny! George's guilty conscience vanished in a great gust of laughter. What a thing to do to the little perisher! Served him right!

Partington however, was as cocky as ever.

'How about it ducky?' he yelled out to Sybil. 'Fancy a night out with Baldy?' and sitting down, he patted his knee.

Sybil's eyes were like saucers. 'Oh, I say, Bertie!' she cried, and rushing round the bar, mini skirt flying, she hopped on his knee and patted his shiny dome. 'Dead sexy!' she breathed.

George's head whirled, but his hands never faltered. They served drinks, took pound notes and gave change like a robot. Out of the corner of his eye he noticed Sybil was back on the job, still laughing and shouting remarks.

'Would you believe it?' she said to George. 'His hair just fell to pieces – came apart in his hands! But doesn't he look better without that wig? I always said so!'

scots pine

Betty was born in Glasgow where she honed her writing skills at the age of eight by writing love letters on behalf of the boy next door. This developed into story writing, the publication of which followed marriage and a shortage of funds.

She has been a valued member of the Circle for many years. Her short stories have been published in Women's magazines and read on Radio 4, but you need to listen to her reading them herself to really appreciate her warmth and wonderful sense of humour.

Dougall Gentles

THE BARD'S TALE

The chieftain had been observing his battle leaders closely as they talked. Vengeance, frustration and thinly disguised apprehension emanated from them. They needed a scapegoat. Nordos knew that it would not be long before they would turn on him if no other outlet could be found for their anger. The serfs had provided the perfect solution.

Nordos spoke, 'We have seen how these peasants defy us with their attacks. We have been too lenient on them and we starve. The gods are angry because of our lack of action and are punishing us by rotting the crops in their fields. Your children go hungry and word from the other clans tell of the same predicament. Although we have offered sacrifice of the peasants on the ritual platform, this is not enough. I have consulted the seer and the dying peasants entrails point to darkness and death. We must attack to ward off this punishment.'

Many of the men rose from their benches shouting approval, the light of battle kindling in their eyes. They had a chance of acquitting themselves well in battle and, with the captured food, each warrior dreamed of winning the hero's portion. This would please the gods and satiate their ingrained love of a fight.

Nordos raised an imperious hand. He had noticed that a few of the warriors were less enthusiastic - they would have to be watched. He made a mental note to put them at the forefront of the raiding party. Hopefully they would be killed in the conflict thus removing any potential dissenters.

'When the sickle moon rises to its zenith we will move like wolves and fight with the ferocity of the boar. Strap your armour close and blacken your faces with clay from the water-pit. We will attack on foot - remember we are after the peasants food - do not kill too many, we still need their puny backs for the fields. We will teach these vermin a lesson they wont forget.'

Cheers rose again as the warriors clamoured in anticipation of the fight. All their lives they had been brought up in the way of the warrior. Childhood rituals marked their transition into adulthood. Not all children survived the physically demanding and dangerous tasks. There was also the spiritual strain for a chosen few of journeys into the realms of the spirits where Jondor the Druid invoked the ancestors. It was said that Jondor could kill or cure with a glance and even Nordos did not dare to challenge him.

Nordos leaned forward and filled his boars head drinking horn with wine. The other warriors watched as he took a long drink wiping the drips from his moustache with the back of his hand. Servants placed a large cooked boar on the table and the onlookers licked their lips in anticipation of the feast. Deliberately, Nordos tore a steaming joint of meat from the boiled boar and began to eat, its juices dripping from his chin. Just as in a wolf pack the dominant male had first choice of the kill so this was the signal for the others to begin eating. Soon little could be heard but the ripping of teeth through tenderised flesh and the gulping of wine. Finally the warriors, satiated, belched their approval.

The wine flagon was passed around again and the war leaders began to boast of the fight to come. Memories of bygone battles prompted the men to relate stories of past glories until as one they clamoured for the Bard.

There was a delay as the servant went out to fetch him. Then he was there trying to remain dignified despite having been almost dragged from the arms of his mate. His ruffled hair and disarrayed clothing did not escape the notice of the warriors particularly as Ayslak was always a meticulous dresser. After a pause the men, encouraged by the wine, burst into laughter and ribald comments. Dignity in tatters, Ayslak fumbled for his harp.

'What would you have me play my Lord?' Ayslak ventured.

'Give us a battle tale Bard,' Nordos replied slurring his words.

Ayslak thought for a moment and then ran his fingers over the instrument. The effect was magical. All heads turned to the sound and there was quiet but for the crackling of burning birchwood.

The Bard's fingers played lightly over the strings of the harp and he watched as the warriors gaze became more distant as the music carried them. He began to sing in a rich, deep and sonorous voice of the ancestral heroes of the Fordwelli. The men around the table were captivated by the melody and the quality of the storyteller's voice.

'Hearken great warriors to the tale I am to tell,' Ayslak began, 'for it is our story and our proud heritage. Wulfrik was our ancestor, great warrior was he, who led our people to victory over other pretenders to this land. Many enemies did he face but none greater than the warriors blond from over the eastern sea. Terrible they were to behold and taller by a full head than many of our men folk. Many skirmishes had been fought until one bright day, with the sun aloft as if to witness the gathered hordes, the enemy stood, their chariots shining in the light, arrayed against the Fordwelli ...'

Transported by the music, the warriors imagined the ranks of their ancestors enemies gathered against Wulfrik the legendary founder of the clan and his warriors. There he stood, feet braced, red hair flowing, ready for combat, surrounded by warriors of great courage and strength.

'With a gesture of command the ancestral Fordwelli began to sing and shout and clash their spears against shield. The noise was fearsome. Then boar-headed battle horns brayed harshly echoing across the defile that lay between the two forces. The enemy tried vainly to match the din.

Suddenly a warrior of the blond-haired force stepped forward clashing sword on bronze shield. A challenge! Many vied for the honour of facing the man in single combat but Wulfrik alone chose to meet him. Unlike his enemy Wulfrik stripped until he stood naked, his body decorated by blue tattoos and the golden Torc about his neck. His muscles bulged underneath silver armlets.

Seizing his bronze sword and shield he ran screaming, hair loosed from its topknot, to meet the contender. Wulfrik stopped short of the challenger and they warily began to circle each other watching for any sign of weakness. Suddenly the challenger swooped, his lunging spear for the Fordwelli's legs. Wulfrik leapt into the air and the spear cut the air harmlessly below his feet. The spear wielder however had unbalanced slightly with the swing and Wulfrik, fleet of foot, brought his sword to bear. Slashing through the air it cut the spear in half. The clans watched as the bronze spear-head spun in the air, glinting in the sun, to imbed itself in the turf.

Recovering, the warriors circled again. Sweat ran down the challenger's face whilst Wulfrik's lean muscled body gleamed in the sunlight. The warriors charged at each other using the boss of their shields as weapons. They met with a resounding crash as bronze clashed with bronze. Both shields buckled under the impact but before the challenger could withdraw, Wulfrik struck with the slashing sword. Such was the strength in the hero's arms that he split the iron mail slicing the flesh just above the hip. Blood sprayed the earth. A great roar of approval rose from the Fordwelli clans and the challenger staggered backward his face contorted with pain.

Wulfrik pressed his advantage hacking and slashing at the shield until the wood beneath the bronze began to splinter. With each blow the challenger's arm weakened but finding hidden strength the clansman rallied and with a great bellow, swung the shield to and fro using its ragged bronze and timber edges as a cutting weapon. Driven back momentarily, Wulfrik redoubled his efforts until the challenger, weakening with loss of blood, staggered backward with each blow. Dodging the slicing shield Wulfrik bent low and lunged forward hamstringing one of his opponent's legs with a slash of his sword. Off balance, the warrior toppled backward and fell, impaled on the jagged haft of his lunging spear lodged in the ground. A great cry escaped his lips echoing in the hills around him. Then he died.

After a silent pause the Fordwelli clans erupted in a cacophony of shouts, cheers and jeers, the battle horns in accompaniment. Wulfrik leant on his long slashing sword getting his breath and then with an elated whoop, bent toward the vanquished champion decapitating him in one stroke. Removing his bronze helm he grasped the enemy warrior by the hair and held its bloody dripping form aloft for all to see. Up went another victory cry from the Fordwelli whilst moans issued from the other side of the defile.

Wulfrik began walking back up the hill towards his comrades when a spear thunked into the ground beside him. More followed the first and soon he found himself dodging. The harsh horns of the enemy clans erupted with a roar of rage from their warriors and chariots and horsemen from both sides spurred their way down to meet in the bottom of the defile. Wulfrik was plucked to safety by a fleet rider and rearmed for the battle.

The two groups of clans fought and fought, the advantage swaying first one way then another until the sun was low in the sky. The earth ran red with blood and the mangled bodies of the dead and dying. Volley upon volley of arrows and spears were thrown by the Fordwelli over the stalemated front where swords and spears bristled in the melee. Gradually they took their toll on the fresher men behind until the foremost enemy warriors weakened under the pressure of Fordwelli warriors. At last the front rank broke and fled except for a few elite warriors defending their chieftain. Each was cut down in turn and Wulfrik engaged the chieftain in single combat. The chieftain fought bravely but to no avail, finally falling prey to Wulfrik's martial skill.

Such a celebration was had that night,' Ayslak continued, 'that men never tired of telling the tale, and it is said that the head of the champion and his chieftain are kept preserved in olive oil by the descendants of Wulfrik in honour of that great victory.'

The battle leaders looked wistful and elated as the last note of the Bard's musical tale faded. Then they erupted with applause with great thumping of fists on the oak table so that the bones of the feast jumped and fell on the floor to be gnawed and fought over by the chieftain's hunting dogs.

Nordos waited for a few moments for all the excitement to die down. Feet braced, leaning on the timber table, he surveyed with satisfaction the faces of his war leaders.

'Go now,' he said 'and prepare yourselves for battle - tonight we will offer sacrifices to the gods of our forefathers!'

Turning swiftly Nordos strode from the hall, cloak swirling behind him.

This piece has been adapted from one chapter of a 'work in progress'. In the novel, as yet untitled, Dougall's story tells of the lives and conflicts of Celtic tribes during the late Iron Age.

douglas fir

Dougall's main interest is in experimental archaeology, in which he has a doctorate. His writing reflects this and benefits from his expertise in this field. He has a long term association with the Forest of Dean.

Rachel Hayward

Witch Hunt Hill

Preceding 1586, Witch Hunt Hill, on the outskirts of Reading in Berkshire, had been formerly known as Little St John's Wood. The hill rose from the banks of the River Thames just above Sonning and covered an area of approximately three miles.

During the latter part of the fourteen hundreds and then, up until 1586 a small village had grown amongst the trees which at its height had a population of just over four hundred and fifty.

For wisdom and guidance the village looked to its Spiritual Leader the Rev. John Parsonage. He was, so records tell, a good and fair man who loved his family and flock equally and, it is therefore sad how the *History of Little St John's Wood* relates the story of his daughter with so little reference to himself and the turmoil he must have felt during this period.

His first child, a daughter, Mary, was born in the spring of 1573. Records tell that although she was said to be a pretty girl she had a slight deformity of the face. Her right eye was noticeably higher than her left. Apparently, even with this she was a happy and contented child. That was until the summer of 1582 when her mother bore a son. It was written that Mary became very jealous of the baby and refused to help her parents with the running of the home in any way.

Then one night when the boy was no more than three months old he kept the household awake for most of the night with his crying. He was inconsolable. In the early hours of the following morning Mary was heard to scream (presumably at her brother) 'Shut up, shut up, shut up. If you don't shut up I'll kill you!'

Presumably the boy was not at all consoled by his sister's words because by daybreak the child was dead.

If Mary was in fact to be blamed for her brother's death, we shall never know but from that day until the tragic events of 1586 every child that Mary's mother bore died before they reached their first birthday. The strange thing was that all seemed to bear the same symptoms. Dark red, swollen blotches would appear on the child's body. These would be accompanied by convulsions of the most violent kind, and also a high fever. After several hours of being in this horrendous state their tiny bodies would turn a dark purple, almost black in colour and they would die. On each occasion Mary would show no signs of grieving or remorse.

The villagers became wary of Mary and her family. People stopped going to church and talk was rife. Mary, they decided, was a witch. It was not long before gossip spread to neighbouring villages and soon it reached the ears of the Head of the Church.

At this time in history the hunting of witches was commonplace and it was not long before the witch-hunters turned up at Little St John,s Wood and interrogated Mary and her family. Of course Mary denied being a witch but in those days it was God to whom you ultimately answered and only He knew the truth.

Mary was tied to the Ducking Stool. This was a strange contraption, which was supposed to prove whether or not you were a witch. You were seated at one end and pivoted round and then ducked into the village pond and told to confess. This was done thirteen times. The innocent drowned. If, however, you survived the ducking you were obviously kept safe by your powers and this was enough evidence to find you guilty of witchcraft.

Mary survived the ducking.

She was taken from the stool and tied to a stake in the centre of the village and burnt as a witch. As the flames leapt at the teenager's legs she screamed out that the village and all those responsible would die.

Strangely no child was ever born to any member of the village after this and eventually the village was lost amongst the trees. To those that lived in Reading and the surrounding towns Little St John's Wood became known as Witch Hunt Hill and it was not until the 1950's that the area became once again used for residential purposes.

There is now a rather exclusive estate on Witch Hunt Hill. The average price for a house is £500,000 and most possess swimming pools and tennis courts. The curse Mary left behind her seems to have worn off with the years, However, Mary made sure that even to this day she was not forgotten.

* * *

July 1st 1986 was a hot and humid day in Berkshire. It was also a Saturday and the children of Witch Hunt Hill had spent the day playing in the shade of the surrounding woodland.

The early evening seemed to bring out the barbeques and it was not long before the residents decided to get together and have one big party. According to all everyone had a great time and there were no misadventures. A fair amount of alcohol was consumed but no one was overly drunk.

By 10pm the barbeques had been extinguished and people were listening to music, drinking and laughing with each other. All children were accounted for.

It was around 1am when someone said they could smell burning. Several others agreed but no source for the acrid smell could be found.

The Gillian family lived at the The Shamrocks, a massive nine-bedroomed house whose kitchen looked out on a large area of grassland in the centre of the estate. Mrs Gillian had popped back into her house via the back door to get another couple of bottles of wine when she happened to glance out through the kitchen window. Her scream was so loud that it brought her husband, a lawyer, and several other male guests from the party rushing in to see what the problem was.

They found her, her hands clasping the kitchen sink, staring out through the window. They followed her gaze and were horrified at what they saw.

44

In the centre of the green appeared to be a large bonfire that was burning furiously. Rising from the fire, they could all see a person attached to a pole of some sort, apparently being burnt alive.

Immediately someone called the emergency services. Within ten minutes the police, fire and ambulance crews had arrived but the bonfire and its burning occupant had mysteriously vanished leaving virtually no trace that the phenomenon had ever been there. All that remained was a circular patch of warm, singed grass.

At first the police took the story as a drunken hoax. But the story from the five men was unwavering. All the men were of good standing within their community and all held places of trust within their chosen career. A surgeon, a lawyer, a retired Detective Inspector, a solicitor, a Member of Parliament and a retired Reverend had witnessed the event and none would change their statement. In the end the Police filed the case away hoping it would be forgotten about.

No such event has occurred since this incident in 1986 but Michael Blake, a researcher into the Paranormal, raised an interesting point.

'The strange connection between the witnesses of the 1986 incident and the burning of Mary in 1586 did not strike me for some time even though it was so obvious it was strangling me. The retired Reverend bore the same name as Mary's father. Unfortunately whether or not they were indeed related we shall never know, as the records of Mary's family seem to stop after 1666.'

Satisfaction Guaranteed

Sandra Heselton, thirty something, single (God, she had to get used to that word), stood back and studied her handiwork as an artist might study a finished canvas. As her eyes took in what she had created she smiled and as the smile turned into a broad grin she realised how long it was since a smile had played across her lips. She was happy. She had succeeded.

Three and a half months ago her long-term partner had decided to start renovations in their dilapidated bathroom. Two weeks after he had ripped everything out she had found him giving dictation to his secretary in a most unsatisfactory manner and so she had ripped him out, of her life, completely.

She had, in the space of twenty-four hours, found herself not only without her soul-mate but also without everything that the soul-mate brought to their relationship: love, companionship, an electrician, a builder, a plumber, a decorator, whilst she, Sandra Heselton, thirty something, well let's just say the last time she picked up a paintbrush was in primary school.

But that, in the space of the last five days had all changed. So far she had changed a fuse in a plug, unblocked the sink and now completely renovated her bathroom. *Her* bathroom and she didn't mind admitting to anyone that would listen, she was bloody proud of the result.

It had all started funnily enough in the bath. She was crying and as she wept some plaster fell into the bath. It wasn't a lot but as she watched the grey flakes sink gently over her knees she had there and then decided that enough was more than enough. Something had to be done. She, Sandra Heselton, thirty something, had to take control.

The following morning, Sandra was outside her local library impatiently waiting for it to open. As soon as the doors were unlocked, Sandra almost ran in and found the section she was looking for. A book entitled 'DIY – So Easy A Child Could Do It' caught her attention and after noting that it had a section on tiling she hired it for the next three weeks. She sat in her car for forty-five minutes reading and re-reading that particular section and was filled with such a feeling of empowerment that she drove home immediately, measured the walls in her bathroom and then drove straight to the large Home Improvements Store just out of town.

Taking her DIY bible in with her she found the bay that held all her tiling requirements and began to load up her trolley with the necessary grout, adhesive, tile cutter, sponge, trowel grouter and squeegee. For that professional finish she also grabbed a box of spacers. Once she had all the technical bits she then turned her attention to what she was most looking forward to – the tiles themselves.

As she moved along the rows of brightly coloured, various shaped and sized tiles it suddenly dawned on her that she really had given no thought to what she actually wanted. Was she searching for the modern, contemporary, antique, farmhouse, or downright wacky look? She was not sure but then something caught her eye. A calming, tranquil, serene design that was everything and more that she could wish for.

Without thinking twice she carefully piled up her trolley with enough tiles to more than cover her bathroom and with a feeling of anticipation and excitement she headed for the check-out till and then home to begin her project.

And so here she was, three days later at ten-thirty in the evening staring in complete rapture at her, yes her completed artwork. All she had to do now was let it dry. Once again she let her eyes wander over her creation, the neatly placed white tiles that framed the peaceful and soothing scene that the centre piece depicted. She had created an island, surrounded by a beautiful, mesmerizing ocean that lapped gently onto golden sands and here and there a seagull playing in the thermals that she could almost feel hovering gracefully over the island.

Feeling the need to celebrate she headed downstairs and opened and then poured herself a large glass of red wine. She let herself chuckle as the thought of not needing to share the wine entered her head and then she headed back upstairs to toast her accomplishment. It was then as she re-entered the bathroom that her face fell and she realised that she had been more than a little premature in her celebrations. She had not completed the job. The walls, yes, they were sublime and the suite, that was good, but the floor, oh yes the floor. She had completely forgotten about the floor. What she was staring at now was a filthy, paint stained, grout encrusted piece of lino. It wouldn't do, it wouldn't do at all.

Feeling slightly dejected but optimistic, she retraced her steps, but instead of entering the kitchen, she went directly into the study and turned on her computer. Once it had warmed up, she entered the words 'interior flooring' into her search engine and waited briefly for the suggestions to come up. There were hundreds of them, thousands in fact, and it was not until she clicked on the fifteenth page that something caught her eye. 'walk-on-water.co.uk', she clicked on the link.

Sandra read on, already convinced that this was the product that would complete her bathroom. Without even bothering to look at the price (money was now no object) she emailed the company requesting a salesman to call. She booked an appointment for the very next day and when the automated email response replied confirming her allotted time for ten o'clock the following morning, she switched the computer off with a feeling of exuberance and elation.

The next day after a virtually sleepless night, Sandra showered and dressed and waited for the company rep to arrive. And right on time, arrive he did. He was much older than Sandra had expected. She always believed that anyone who had anything to do with internet companies would be no older than twenty, covered in spots and wearing thick rimmed glasses. But this gentleman was closer to forty and very presentable. After their introductions he followed Sandra into the bathroom and immediately set to work measuring the floor space. It was only after he had completed the task that he came downstairs and accepted Sandra's offer of a cup of tea.

'You know this won't be cheap?' he asked, staring directly at Sandra.

'Go on,' she prompted. 'Give me the worst.'

'Two thousand, five hundred pounds!'

'When can you fit it?'

'If I ring these measurements through now and you give me the cheque, within three days.'

'There is just one thing,' the sales rep said hesitantly. 'We have had some unusual reports back from some of our customers, not that we've been able to verify them, but some people have said they have found it a little too realistic.'

'In what way?' enquired Sandra.

'People have said that they have seen things in the lino, things we haven't put there.'

Sandra raised an inquisitive eyebrow.

The salesman shifted uncomfortably in his seat. 'Fish!' he replied to her unspoken question.

Sandra smiled and handed him the cheque. 'I like fish,' she said.

Three days later, Sandra was staring at her bathroom floor a little apprehensively. She knew it was only lino but … it looked nothing like any lino she had ever seen. It rippled and shimmered and she could swear that she could see depth. It was as if she had her own private ocean right there in her bathroom. She put her toes out and touched it gently, half expecting to get them wet, but no, the floor was hard. She lowered her foot down and took one tentative step and then another. It was true. It was as if she was walking on water. She shrieked with delight. Her bathroom was finally completed.

It was three nights later when something caught her eye,

although in truth, she could not say exactly what it was. As she was cleaning her teeth before bed, she swore she saw a dark shadow glide below the surface of the lino, but when she looked again there was nothing there. Shaking her head and smiling to herself, she switched off the light and went to bed.

The following morning she awoke to the sound of the bin men collecting a mound of rubbish from outside her home and as she lay huddled under the covers, a feeling of disappointment swept over her. Her project was finished and she had given no thought to any other. This notion was still with her as she rose from her bed and wandered into her bathroom for her morning ablutions.

Maybe because of the early morning and the fact that she was still half asleep, or maybe because she was simply not prepared for what she saw, Sandra stood for over three minutes staring by the bathroom door. She could not believe what she was seeing. It was as if someone had come in during the night with several buckets of water and just hurled them everywhere. The sink was full even though she was positive she had emptied it. There was water pooled on the window sill – and as for the bath. Unable to make either head or tail of it she went downstairs for a cloth to clear up the mess. Returning and wiping everything down her mind raced as to what or who could have caused this watery disarray and without thinking she wiped the back of her hand across her mouth and she licked her fingers. She licked her lips, realising that she needed a cup of tea and, she tasted – salt! She licked her fingers again and this time she could taste the strong alkaline flavour. This was too bizarre. She sat back by the bathroom door and tried to think.

It was then that the answer came to her as she watched the reason for the bathroom chaos glide purposefully upwards through the murky depths, then, as it neared the surface, turn and head back down, Sandra realised she had a problem, a big problem.

Still staring into her now empty ocean, Sandra tried to make some equations. The sales rep had said that some owners of this lino had reported seeing fish, but she presumed he had meant little, friendly fish, not bloody great big, huge, enormous dangerous fish. And then there was the water. Could this bloody great big, huge, enormous, dangerous fish actually break through the water and cause the flood in her bathroom? Well, as the water wasn't real (but it was), the fish wasn't real (but it looked real), then the logical answer would be no. Her head still swimming with non-equating equations, Sandra went to find tea.

Sandra sat staring at her tea blankly with absolutely no idea of any explanation for the series of events that had befallen her, when her thoughts were interrupted by her doorbell. Still in somewhat of a daze, she stood up and slowly walked to the door and opened it. The day could not get any worse.

'What do you want?' she asked tersely.

'Can I come in?' and before she realised what she had done, she nodded and let the ex-boyfriend from hell enter.

'I made a huge mistake. I'm so sorry. Can we try again please?' Sandra shrugged. She had other things, more important things to think about right now. This was just not a good time but she did not have the energy to send him away. It was then that she realised that he was still talking and as she listened, a plan began to form in her mind.

'... I can't believe what a bastard I was, and leaving the bathroom like that, I know it was unforgivable of me ...'

'Oh I've done the bathroom,' Sandra interrupted. 'Why don't you go and have a look? See what you think.'

The ex-boyfriend from hell stared at her in disbelief. 'But you couldn't ...'

'I had no choice,' she said, 'Go on, go and have a look.'

He rose and headed up the stairs. 'Do you mind if I use the toilet while I'm up here?' he called down.

'No, help yourself.' She replied.

There were a couple of seconds silence and then a

'BLOODY HELL! Can I walk on this?' Followed by a 'This is brilliant!' Then she heard the door close and the toilet seat being lifted up. Then there was silence.

The silence seemed to go on endlessly, but in reality it was only for a minute as it was then broken by the sound of him flushing the toilet. Sandra waited for him to open the door, but the sound never came. She waited some more but still nothing. After half an hour she slowly rose from her seat and went upstairs.

The door was still closed and she pushed it slowly, not really sure what she was expecting to see. As the door opened to its full extent, Sandra surveyed the bathroom. Again there was water everywhere, up the walls, in the sink and bath and dripping down the window, but as to the ex-boyfriend from hell, well he was nowhere to be seen. There was, however, a large chunk missing from the toilet seat, almost as if something had risen out of the fathoms and taken a large bite out of it.

Sandra sighed somewhat sadly and went back downstairs to make a phone call, but as she was dialling the number for 'walk-on-water.co.uk' she replaced the handset and smiled. How in all honesty could she tell them that she was not one hundred percent happy with her new floor? After all, she had just had her satisfaction guaranteed!

sugar maple

Rachel is a long-term member and has been the Circle's Chairman for a total of nine years. She is currently in that position. She has written two novels and numerous short stories, even breaking into verse on occasions. Her work veers towards the macabre.

Julian Horsfield

Kitchen Sink
(I'll liberate you later)

I slip the Marigolds on me fingers
listening to the fifties swingers,
filling the bowl and chucking in plates,
chewing a sickly After Eight –
lots of baked on grease today
tasted lishious – I should say!
Lots of swimming slimy cups
how I love the washing ups!
Brace yourself, time to be bold
tip in coffee that went cold,
squeeze the bottle in the sink
water right up to the brink,
here's a laugh, here's a joke,
every day I have to cope,
with the plug-hole flipping choked.
Bits of egg and pasta shells
most perculiar onion smells.
How I'd love something to wash –
a nice machine perhaps by Bosch,
something making washing sounds
as I melt the Marigolds down …
Until then I'll have to dream
rub in lashings of Atrixo cream –
If I ever had a wish
a nice and easy ovenproof dish
Would be high up on my list –
that and a Brillo with a bit of life,
God it would be awful nice
to have a nineteen-fifties wife.

Forest Girls

'em dun as giggle much,
but like as their tits squeezed
if ems a good'un.
But ums prone to pregnancy
round here as yung uns.
So allas wear a johnny if
thou doesn't want to fetch
em down the aisle.
Young Beryl's a prime gal
her comes from Ruardean
and married a boy from Blaisdon
so as she could get her hands
on his plums.
'im worked at Ranks till
'em Yanks shut up shop.
He's resting now, on the social
butty, and she's got a nipper-
as do call 'em rugrats.
Take Lillian, her's another
from Cinderford – udnt be
the first – her had fifteen kids
and is still smiling, her old man
worked on production line
at Beechams, we was always
commenting must be the blackcurrants
as makes 'im so randy.
Ay 'em's good girls round here, but
as I said, 'em's prone to pregnancy
as yung uns so allas wear a Johnny.

Mother's Day

You tend to the dying,
I will wash the floors,
I will black the boots,
you empty the ash from the fire,
Eric, tend those weeds at the front
and I will cook the ham.
Brenda, go to the village
and bring back some coal
in the cart,
Eric, dress Grandfather in
a clean white shirt.
Susie, come down stairs
and see if there's any mushrooms
to make a rabbit pie with,
I will spread the table, and trim
the wax, Eric, you know what to do,
so why sit back?
Aunt Agnes isn't well or I'd have
her helping at the stove,
and Eric, after you've tended
the weeds, find some marigolds
to put in a vase.
John is mending the clocks
at his work in the shed,
I, am now going to sit down
for five minutes and have
a well earned rest.

The Apple

And in his hand an apple round and red
such gravity occurred within his head,
First saw the world a spinning ball
towards the which all objects fall.

Yet once before and ere the dawn
in Paradise was Adam born,
Where russet grew and tasted sweet
no longer did the promise keep.

Scientist or priest it's in the bite
the seeming of the raying light,
The essence of this mystery
is formed in doubting history.

Yet had it blight or never dropped
The fruit not many laden cropped,
How much of life had come to be
Lest Eve or Isaac first found that tree?

An Image of William Wordsworth

Wondering if I wander,
O'er hills and valleys, alone
like a cloud, wondering where
I go to next, blown by the winds
of fleeting thoughts. The famous words
of a past poet,
bring an image, graceful, floating.

And that cloud was filled with air
by the breath of a breathing man,
who moved me, once, and once again
over the skies of my more jubilant days.
Oh! To be free! In England!
This start of June, is peaceful, and
tranquil in the woods, my dog beside
me on the trail, all of the places
I revisit, are steeped in spirit, I sit alone
with a book of Wordsworth, at a secret spot
and eat my picnic, shared with the dog.

And the loneliness is loveliness,
my thoughts moving alone,
considering the landscape of the vales
and hills, and hosts of golden daffodils.
Those tuned and honed words of love
spread wings of wisdom, down the years,
in vibrating notes of song and solitude,
I continue to embrace and be filled
with William's words.

He wandered here, in
The Dean forest and fields,
considering a love for this nature,
that we share, (those who walk the dyke
and see the abbey, at Tintern,
in the Wye Valley). And then he returned
again, drawn in mystery and revery,
to write his wondrous poetry.
God gave the man his measure, and his
rhymes, his work immortal, and sublime.

Morning Light

Do I appear devoted to this shining ball
that balances and rises in thin air?
Am I a worshipper of this golden sun
no greater thing within plain sight?
Though mountains move and slowly rise
no morning cloud can reach.
It is God's kindness to the world,
His salient light upon the mind,
that fills us with such grace.

The Rose

By any other name is sweet*
True lovers own that love is deep.
I see a fever and less repose
the maddening redness of a rose,
I see enchantment and a grave
a white and lasting purity.
The dew encrusted petals meet
around each heart as love is sworn.

Grasped in hand so drawing
blood the thorns bite deeper into flesh
Entwined arms and lips are meet
in service to the budding rose.
The fragrance intoxication brings
and onto fingers golden rings.
The gothic spires dream only of this;
To die and be revived with just a kiss.

The Kiss

Such lips in trembling first embrace
as tongues are touching moistly taste,
the living tip is warm and free
to shape and twist most joyfully.
It's to the mind we know of love
and melt delicious into this.
Happiness is soon achieved:
Here is the sweet desired Kiss.

In colours complex to describe
clasped in awe with closed eyes.
We sometimes may just take a peep
to see the blissful brows so crease.
Those tender eyes speak needfully
to be so cherished in this disease.
That flame once kindled can be unkind
to flicker fortune's favour blind.

* Line taken from William Shakespeare.

In the Beginning

Before the fall in acres wild
before Eve's first and lonely child
Before the flood or might of kings
Before the dawn creation brings
Was in that nature God alone
and in himself complete.
Unending and in splendid power
no which, no what, just all in all
'till hands flung stars and time grew tall.

briar rose

Julian says that some of his happiest moments have occurred on mornings armed with a coffee and word processor, staring into space. He has few ambitions, apart from getting together a book of poetry.

Another Member

KINGS OF THE ROAD

Why this long tailback?
What's causing the drawback
On this particular road?
Are they shifting a circus?
A nuclear reactor?
No, it's a farmer up on his tractor
Hauling his vegetable load.

The view is quite fine
And we've got the time
To take in its autumnal grace.
Strolls the laud of this landscape?
His ghillie?
His factor?
No, it's a farmer up on his tractor
Keeping us all in our place.

Why this slow panorama?
Is there some sort of drama-
A matter of surgical skill?
Have they mislaid the forceps?
The scalpel?
Retractor?
No, it's a farmer up on his tractor
Making us feel this ill.

Could it be an infection
That detains this collection
Of desperate road-tax displayers?
A virus? A fungus?
A helicobacter?
No, it's some farmer up on his tractor
Who holds back these people-conveyors.

In this remote shire
Is there danger about
From an animal wild and ferocious?
Is it a herbivore?
Is it a raptor?
No, there's a farmer out with his tractor
At the speed of a tired diplodocus.

Are they making a movie,
A weepie, a thriller?
Some sort of commercial promotion?
Is that a policeman
Or is he an actor?
No, it's that farmer up on his tractor
Driving this road in slow motion.

Is an Alternative Medic at work up ahead
Who's causing my back to go numb?
A wild osteopathist?
A tame chiropractor?
No, it's our farmer out with his tractor
Stretching this supinal column

.

Architect with protractor
And building contractor
Would both thump him hard till he squealed-
But look!
This wurzel extractor
On supercharged tractor
Is now speeding across his own field,
And at last the traffic's free-wheeled, my friends,
At last the traffic's free-wheeled.

Empty Garage Syndrome

I have just been out to the garage. The night is very cold, but I just had to check. When I unlocked the door the garage was empty, still empty. No denying it. My lovely Lada has gone. Its empty space not speaking to me, only oil in the centre of the floor to remind of its late occupant. I leave the plastic bag full of its retrieved little possessions, switch off the light to relock the door.

Silly to mourn the demise of a car, but this was a car which, for all the trouble it gave me, I had become attached to and, it has gone, not to another good home, but to the breakers yard, where even now it must be mystified to be standing among a bunch of strange cars on such a chilly night.

I had bought the car thirteen years ago when I spotted it on a local garage forecourt, its long red roof being the right length on which to lower down the heavy Canadian canoe from its storage place under the garage roof. Held by ropes and pulleys it is easily inched down onto the roof-rack of a car. But lately we have not used the canoe or completed a proposed voyage down the river Severn, now maybe we never will.

I was only the second owner when I bought the car in 1994 when it had already done thirty-eight thousand miles and had a number of minor faults which Thompson's garage fixed when I found them out driving in the first few days. I do not do a high mileage and in those thirteen years I have never done more than four thousand five hundred miles in any year and indeed in the last three years never more than two thousand eight hundred. But its ailments have been growing relentlessly, for example its headlights had the habit of going right out instead of dipping, leading to heart-stopping moments when another comes at you with lights blazing – and leaving you in complete darkness when it has passed and you find the hedge but milli-seconds away.

The brakes also failed when going down Rodborough Hill

recently on the way to a Local History Symposium in Stroud Museum. I managed to go down the gears to bring the car to a halt where the road joins the Stroud-Bath main road as there was some braking function left but had to leave Ruth at the mid-session interval and hurry into town to buy a bottle of brake fluid at Halfords. This full bottle stands now on the garage shelf like the bottle of medicine a dying person leaves by their bedside.

For just before Christmas the car had its annual MOT and a horrendous number of faults were found including, 'offside suspension mounting prescribed area excessively corroded. 'Dangerous!' Front brake application uneven 'Dangerous!' and six other faults either dangerous or below requirements. And! 'I certify, for the reasons above the vehicle was not shown to comply with the statutory requirements.'

My garage man said he really couldn't save it another time. 'Ring up Forest Auto Salvage, Cinderford. They'll take it away for free.' Before backing it out I emptied its little treasures from the glove shelf.

Looking over them now I have found tickets to park at St Columb Town Council's Recreation Ground in Cornwall, Bourton Vale Park and Warwick Castle. As well there are two folding cups, three unopened packets of Kleenex, a spare rear-view mirror, and (whisper it not,) a flake of spotted Dolerite of which the Stonehenge inner circle is made.

When the car breaker man arrived he was not the youth I had spoken to on the phone, but a solemn, middle aged man who acted with all the professional dignity of an undertaker come to collect the body. All I had to do was sign a form which he filled out to post to the DVLA in Swansea. He would do the rest. He was particularly pleased when I told him he could just back the car out. 'And here are the keys' I said. 'I don't think I can watch.'

But I did of course, from a room overlooking the road. Already aboard his truck was a car which he pumped up to an alarming angle. He then got into the Lada and drove it up the steep ramp with such a flourish it made me proud at the noise of its engine. The car was as innocent as an old stallion on its way to the knackers yard.

One of my friends who came in said, 'Shall I get you a paper hanky? I know how you feel.' He left me alone in deference to my emotion.

I should have taken my cap off when the cortege came past the house. But I didn't. It was only a defunct old dead car. But that space in the garage? It does need filling!

The Native

This is my spot upon the earth.
This is the land that gave me birth.
You may not love or honour me,
Here was I born and here I be.

red oak (autumn)

'Another Member' has always maintained his anonymity to encourage other shy people, who may not wish to have their names published, to still be brave enough to come and see who we are.
As one of the original members of the Dean Writers' Circle, he enjoys the distinction of rarity.

67

Jackie Orman

THE TALISMAN

Sally Brown checked carefully that she had the borrowed chapel keys in her handbag before locking her front door and glanced at the windows. They were all shut and behind them she could see the glass ball that was her talisman. Steve had given it to her two months before he had disappeared following a savage beating from his father. That must have been a dozen years ago. She had walked out six months later carrying the glass ball and little else and had gone to a women's refuge. From there she had rebuilt her life so that now she owned the trim bungalow with its colourful garden. She had always kept the glass ball in the hope that somehow it would bring the son she had lost back to her.

'Enough of memories,' she thought abruptly and turned to the garden. 'Which flowers would be best for an anniversary?' She picked an armful, put them on the front seat of her car and drove away to arrange them and do her share of chapel cleaning. Round a bend in the lane she passed a group of teenagers in school uniform whispering together and glancing furtively around. Truants from the comprehensive half a mile away, most likely. A group of them had plagued the village for some time now while the school appeared to be doing nothing about the problem.

It was lunch time when she returned. She opened her car door and stared in horror. The garden had been trampled as if by a herd of elephants. Her dustbin had been thrown in the pond so that pieces of rubbish now floated among the water lily leaves. Every window in the bungalow and every pane of glass in the greenhouse had been smashed and the greenhouse staging overturned. Plants and their broken pots lay strewn everywhere. She could even see the thermometer lying among the debris. On the white painted front door was an outline of the Cerne Giant sketched in what looked like a mixture of felt tip and lipstick. A plastic bottle, it looked like a cider bottle, had been taped over the

69

crudely drawn penis with insulation tape – oh God did that mean they had been inside too? One of the window frames swung wide and an assortment of dirty footprints on the sill confirmed her fears.

Inside, the chaos was as great as outside. Furniture had been overturned, drawers emptied. The kitchen floor was awash with smashed eggs and milk from broken bottles. She almost trod on the kitchen timer lying in the doorway along with the remains of the plates from the dresser. In the bedroom clothes and dressing table contents were scattered everywhere. The bathroom revealed that the washbasin had been pulled away from the wall and the bath contained the toilet seat and a mixture of sodden towels and toilet paper. She turned the taps off to stop any more water flooding the floor. The sitting room contained most of the glass from the windows and several ruined ornaments and books. CDs and furniture had been tossed everywhere. An open spectacle case containing a mangled pair of glasses lay in the middle of the room, probably stamped on. After all, it looked as if they had been trampolining on her bed – at least until one of them had been sick in the middle of it. Suddenly she realised her talisman was gone and that some of the glass fragments were curved. It was shattered into tiny pieces, too small even to find, let alone repair. Beyond tears, she leant against the overturned table and covered her face with her hands to shut out the devastation.

Moments later fury exploded within her. How dare they wreck the house and garden – the whole new life she had built by hard work from the ashes of a bad marriage? Mindless vandals almost certainly drunk on cheap cider and probably high on drugs as well! How dare they smash up her house and especially the only link she had with her missing son? By God, she would do all she could to see that they or preferably the parents that had spawned them paid for the damage.

Clearheaded now, she looked round for the telephone. By a miracle it had fallen among a heap of cushions and was undamaged. The police would be best placed to find the culprits. After an apparently interminable wait, she described the state of her home to the duty sergeant, who promised to send an officer as soon as possible, and rang off. The police station was five miles away so she knew it would take at least several minutes before the promised help came. Aware that her wafer thin self control was liable to snap at any moment, she dared not be idle. She decided that an inventory of the damage might help the police, so she picked a writing pad out of the debris surrounding her bureau, found a pen in her handbag and set to work. She must not touch anything, of course, not even that apparently foreign coin inside the window which must have fallen out of a pocket as they climbed through. She wanted the police to have every possible clue that might lead them to the perpetrators.

She was assessing the damage to her garden when the police car turned into her drive. She turned towards it as a tall policeman, his face shaded by his cap, climbed out and began to walk towards the front door. When he saw her, to her surprise, he stopped and stared apparently in astonishment. 'Mrs Sally Brown,' he enquired in a strained voice, 'that used to be Sally Joiner?'

'Yes,' she replied equally surprised.

He took off his cap revealing a shock of light brown hair and blue grey eyes. 'Don't you recognise me?'

'Steve,' she whispered, rooted to the spot, sure she must be dreaming and would wake up at any moment.

His face fell. 'Aren't you glad to see me?'

The well remembered expression broke the spell. 'Steve,oh Steve!' She ran towards him. 'I can't begin to tell you how glad I am. After all these years. It's just – well after the shock I've already had this morning, I thought I must be seeing things. Is it really you and I'm not dreaming?'

He gave her a bear like hug. 'There – that's real enough isn't it? But you certainly do look as if you had seen a ghost. You'd better come and sit down and I'll make you a cup of tea.'

She allowed herself to be guided into the house where Steve turned an armchair the right way up and she sank into it watching his every movement until he left the room to find the kitchen. He returned in a few minutes looking grim and carrying a glass of water.

'Sorry, this is the best I could do,' he apologised. 'At least I managed to find one intact glass. If you'll excuse me for a few minutes I need to call the station. I can't handle this myself – too much risk I'd do the bastards who did this to you some serious harm. It shouldn't be a problem. I was about to go off duty when you rang and only did the call because Serge said you sounded extremely upset. I won't be long.'

'Why not use my phone? I simply don't want to let you out of my sight.'

'Thanks, but I think this is better done on my car radio. You needn't worry – I'm not about to run away again – I've been looking for you for the past five years. You covered your tracks remarkably well.'

'I needed to. Your father threatened that he'd find and kill me if I ever left him.'

She sat nursing her glass of water as Steve left to make his call. She looked at the chaos around her and a glint caught her eye. A small curved piece of glass was catching the sunlight. It would take a lot of time, money and effort to restore her home – if indeed she wanted to continue to live in this violated house, but that didn't matter much at the moment. Her precious ball – her talisman – was broken into a thousand pieces but in breaking, it had brought the son she had despaired of ever seeing again back into her life.

Halloween

'Trick or treat, mister?'

The old man opened the door wider, regarding the caller with interest as a cat might study a mouse. He smiled slowly, revealing yellow uneven teeth. 'Treat of course, my dear. But do come in for a moment while I find something for you. You must be cold standing on the step.' He stood aside as the small figure in the grotesque mask crossed the threshold, then closed the door silently.

A number of people nearby heard a loud shriek but as a group of children dressed in weird costumes were playing in the street at the time no one took much notice. It was several days before anyone checked the old man's house. He lay flat on his back in the hallway, eyes and mouth wide in a silent scream.

The pathologist's report described the wound in his neck as resembling '… a bite, possibly that of a large cat, with several deep punctures one of which penetrated the internal jugular vein,' and gave the cause of death as heart failure apparently brought on by fear and loss of blood.

Loveless Children

Loveless children don't cry.
When no one takes any notice
Why waste your strength and time
On pointless tears?

Loveless children don't speak.
If no one believes what you say
And it only makes matters worse
Why say anything?

Loveless children don't try.
When all you do is criticized,
Or ignored, there's no point
In doing well.

Loveless children don't grow.
They are like seedlings
In a pot no one bothers to water,
Which finally die.

willow

Jackie is retired and lives in Ruardean with her husband and Thomas, a large tabby cat. She has been writing for as long as she can remember, mostly short stories and poetry, but is currently working on a novel.

Anthony Reeve

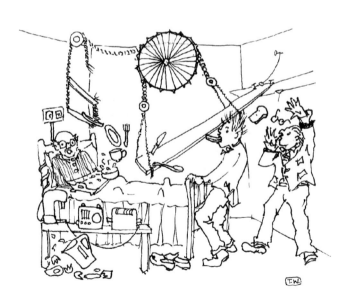

75

THE BREAKFORBED MACHINE

Ever since our honeymoon Angelina had brought me my breakfast in bed, but now she is gone I have to get it myself, a situation which until recently was most satisfactory. Then one morning I received by post an invitation to enter a competition the top prize for which was £75,000. The object of the exercise was to invent a means of making life easier and which would have appealed to, of all people, Heath Robinson. I read the rules of the Heath Robinson award Scheme time and time again until I knew them by heart. I decided to enter the competition and sent off the application form together with the entrance fee. I needed a machine which would replace Angelina to the effect that it would serve me breakfast in bed; so I invented a most unwieldy labour-saving contraption which I called my BREAKFORBED MACHINE.

The competition rules permitted the use of a number of items already invented provided they each formed only a part of the project. Bearing this in mind I utilized an automatic Teasmade which would switch on the radio, the kettle, and the toaster at the appropriate time. I fixed a shelf to the wall near the foot of my bed, and from the shelf I positioned a slide leading down to where a tray would be if I was sitting up in bed. I installed a miniature lift suspended from the ceiling above the head of my bed. The shelf was pivoted in the middle so that any flying object hitting the wall and rebounding onto it would cause it to tip forwards. This motion would operate a switch to activate the lift, and would also allow the flying object to glide smoothly down the slide. The toaster, which was to play a significant part in the proceedings, I connected to the Teasmade to ensure it operated at the right time, and after much trial and error I eventually positioned it for correctness of trajectory. For many weeks I toiled on my BREAKFORBED until, at last, I was in a position to try it out. I set everything ready the night before, and, in the morning it obediently sprang into action.

At the appointed hour, the radio came on, together with the toaster, and the kettle. The timing was perfect. While the kettle was pouring boiling water into the teapot, two slices of toast jumped out from the toaster, flew across the room, hit the wall and fell onto the shelf which pivoted forwards and in doing so operated the switch which put the lift into motion. The lift brought down plate, cup, saucer, bowl, cornflakes, milk, marmalade, butter, two egg cups, knife, fork, spoon; and as I took the plate from the lift, the two slices of toast came sliding onto it. I removed the two boiled eggs from the kettle, and enjoyed the best breakfast I had ever made.

After several days of enjoying breakfast in bed, I was confident my BREAKFORBED was ready for examination by the Heath-Robinson Award Scheme Adjudicators. The day before they came, however, the toaster developed a fault. I did have another toaster, so I swapped the two over and thought no more about it.

I was dutifully lying in bed as the radio came on while the Adjudicators, in deference to whom I switched the radio off, examined the proceedings from my bedside. They waited patiently for the kettle to boil, and as it did so, the two slices of toast came flying across the room from the toaster. But it was not the right toaster; it had not got the right trajectory. One slice of toast hit the shelf and switched the lift on, but the second slice switched it off. The lift stopped with a jerk and blew a fuse in the Teasmade. Plate, cup, saucer, bowl, cornflakes, milk, marmalade, butter, two egg cups, knife, fork and spoon all came tumbling onto my bed. The two slices of toast flew off in different directions with the result one of the Adjudicators had his glasses knocked off while another got his mouth wedged open. The kettle fell on the floor and both eggs smashed inside it.

Needless to say, I did not win the £75,000 top prize. Instead the Adjudicators awarded me a Certificate of Endeavour, neatly framed, and in their accompanying letter they politely suggested I get out of bed and make my own breakfast in the normal way. Fortunately, I have only two days left for this sort of drudgery, for then Angelina returns from visiting her sister in New Zealand. Then, at last, all will he back to normal: Angelina will be bringing in my Breakfast in Bed. I often wonder what Heath Robinson would have thought about my invention - my BREAKFORBED MACHINE.

MISS DOROTHY MOORE

When I left the Royal Air force in 1965 I managed to gain employment as a Civil Servant in the Ministry of Defence, where I was employed in the field of telecommunications, for which I had been trained in the RAF. For a while I maintained contact with two girl friends in the Army, one in the Navy and several in the RAF, but gradually contact was lost with them all and I hit on the idea of advertising for a new girl friend. There was a dating agency by name of Autodates with whom I registered my particulars, including the type of girl I was looking for. I had got used to girls chasing me; arranging via an agency to meet a new girl was a new approach. In due course, however, Autodates sent me details of six girls who they numbered one to six.

I did not like the sound, nor the photograph, of number One, Sarah Wilkins. She reminded me of a female Warrant Officer I had met in the RAF, a beast in a skirt. Number Two, Mary Fields, appeared to be better. We arranged to meet but we soon discovered Autodates had not made a very good match there, so we bade our goodbyes and departed. Number Three, Vivienne Morpeth, confined herself to writing letters in which she was always complaining, not about what I had said in my letters but about what I had not said. I soon got fed up with her. Number Four, Frances Brown, was a dead loss. She never replied to my letter. Number five was a lady from Wiltshire called Dorothy Moore. Number Six, Veronica Saltash, wrote saying she had already found her one and only and wished me best of luck. She sent me a four-leaf clover – which I still have – as a sign of good luck for the future. It was Number Five, therefore, who became my girl friend for the following six years: Miss Dorothy Moore.

Miss Dorothy Moore was a comely wench, a girl with plenty of flesh on her in all the right places, very appealing to men who like their girls to be well formed. She was five feet tall. She had fair hair, blue eyes, and she had an unusually good nature. She was always ready and willing to comply with any decent suggestion. She was able to see the funny side of any indecent suggestion. She was always polite and cheerful; she had a most pleasant smile and she soon became popular with my family and friends. She was a pleasure to be with.

Dorothy was just right for me. From the start, as the saying goes, we got on like a house on fire. She had a house in Greenford, Middlesex, which she rented so she could be near her work. Her family home was in Wilton, Wiltshire, where she would often invite me to spend the weekend with her. My home was Ewell, near Epsom in Surrey, to which she often came. We went on holidays to Gloucestershire, where my Mother's sister, old Auntie Floss, was then living in Little Dean. From there we travelled all over the West Country on holidays.

On the road from Lydbrook to Ross-on-Wye there is a place called Walford where we arrived rather late one evening. The Walford House Hotel had only one vacancy that night and that was a room with a double bed. The thought of this made Dorothy wince. Realizing that it was either this room or the car, she chose the room. It was there I discovered she had a mole just above her navel. There was a wart some distance up her left leg. It amused her every time she felt the scar where I had once had an abcess.

79

Without going into too much detail, suffice to say that that was the night we really got to know each other well.

At home, we spent every available moment meeting here, going there, and generally having a good time. She was a film technician by trade, she knew a number of well known actors and film stars, she was very fond of visiting cinemas and she had albums of photographs of the venues she had been to when on tours overseas with film companies and of places she had visited when on holiday abroad.

We spent considerable time contemplating marriage. This was the reason we finally split up. Dorothy would have been happy to raise a family but she said she preferred to remain what she called a 'free spirit' while I was not prepared to become a father without first being a husband. When I pressed her on the subject, she said she wanted time to think about it. By then we had known one another for six years. She was pleading for more time, not because she needed it but because she did not like to say NO. I asked her how much more time she would require before she was able to say YES. She said she did not know. We let the matter drop.

One day in 1974, we met in Kingston-upon-Thames by previous arrangement. We went to the cinema. Then I took her back to the railway station where we had a cup of coffee in the station buffet. When the train came in I saw her off on her journey back home. We never met again.

Outside the Walford Hotel

DRIVING LESSONS

Many years ago in the Royal Air Force, in those dim and distant days when I was dashing, daring and debonair, I embarked upon an adventure which I still recall, for it is as clear to me now after all these years as it was frightening at the time. Padre Williams set himself up as our Driving Instructor. He would not provide tuition for the Driving Test, he would instead prepare us for our 'exciting journey on the road ahead through life'. No matter how *exciting* he envisaged our journey through life was going to be, the Driving Lesson intended to prepare us for it was positively *frightening*.

There are two similar Driving Lessons which I have to tell concerning my two friends, Peter Robinson and Robin Hilliard, which I shall relate just as they were told to me. First, however, is the account of my Driving Lesson, the starting point of which was the Station Church.

I was soon to imagine the finishing point would be the Station Cemetery. Padre Williams brought from the Scrap Yard a 45-seater single-decker RAF coach. This thing was totally unfit for the public road. Three steps by the door fell away from the bodywork as I scrambled aboard. 'Take over,' said Padre Williams, throwing the steps into the back of the coach. Wing mirrors are essential when driving a bus for the interior mirror cannot be used when reversing. This was just as well, for there was no interior mirror. Having been on duty earlier in the day, I was still wearing RAF uniform including RAF shoes. Because of this I was acutely aware the pedals were too close together; a disadvantage which was to have effect almost immediately.

When I got the engine started the Padre told me to drive the bus to the airfield. To do this I had to 'double declutch', a cumbersome manoeuvre involving all gear changes to be via neutral. I asked him if we were going out onto the public road. 'Good Heavens No! I wouldn't dare!' he exclaimed. When we reached the Control Tower he told me to stop and switch the engine off. He then commenced his Driving Tuition: 'Just as St Peter sank into the water the moment his faith weakened, so you will sink into the abyss should your faith weaken. Therefore you must keep your faith. You have already shown you have some faith by your recent experience in a glider. Today you will need more faith than ever, for you do not know what is going to happen out there. Get moving.' As I switched on the engine, I noticed movement in the Control Tower. This was unusual for there was normally no flying programme on a Sunday. I did hope that everything was under control, but I said nothing. I engaged first gear, after a bit of a struggle, and moved the bus onto the perimeter track.

There were no aircraft about to take off, therefore because of activity in the Control Tower I presumed an aircraft must be coming in to land. If that were so, I thought, then I should not be driving a bus along the perimeter track. I was about to stop to wait for the plane to land when the Padre told me to keep going. 'Accelerate and get across the runway first,' he instructed. I changed down a gear and slammed down on the accelerator hoping it wouldn't go through the floorboards. The bus responded faster than I thought it would. With the increased speed I put it back into top gear, but as I did so I became aware of a fault in the steering. The bus veered over the grass towards the runway. 'Slow down!' called the Padre. 'If we hit the runway we will hit the plane!' I could not slow down. The pedals were too close together. My right shoe had got wedged between accelerator and footbrake, preventing me from releasing the accelerator. The bus was racing towards the runway with the steering now out of control. I put my left foot on the brake but my right foot prevented me from operating it. I grabbed hold of the handbrake, but it came away in my hand, so I threw it through the window. Instead of coming to my rescue, Padre Williams offered me a cigarette.

'How could I possibly smoke now?' I yelled. At last I

managed to pull my right foot free. I immediately jammed on the brakes: but the brakes wouldn't work: the bus kept racing along. Not only did the bus have no steering, it had no brakes. The brake pedal remained on the floor. It would not come up again. I saw a man frantically waving at us from the control Tower. They fired a red flare at us, to keep us off the runway.

A fire engine came racing towards us. Hopelessly out of control, the bus careered onto the runway, and to my abject horror, we were now travelling *along* the runway instead of *across* it. The situation was desperate: no steering - no footbrake - no handbrake - no mirror - no steps. 'The bus is out of control!' I yelled. 'An aerodrome is a large area,' replied the Padre. 'You haven't hit anything yet.' I saw the man still waving at us from the Control Tower. 'The Good Lord above will bring us to a standstill.' said the Padre. 'I hope not - not yet!' I called back in panic. 'Let God get us off the runway first.' 'That will not be necessary,' replied the Padre. 'You have had your Driving Lesson now. We have run out of time.' At that precise moment the bus ran out of fuel. The wretched thing, still in gear, came juddering to a standstill on the runway. There was a long pause. The Crash - the Fire - the Explosion, as the plane hit the coach - never came. I switched off the engine, turned to Padre Williams and gratefully accepted that cigarette he had offered.

No aircraft had been expected that day. Had an unscheduled aircraft arrived the Control Tower would have fired two red flares at us and that would have been the signal. In the event they fired only one. The purpose of the fire engine was to give the impression of impending danger that its presence would inspire; after which it would tow the old bus to the Transport Depot. Padre Williams, with official approval, had arranged the entire scenario beforehand. He knew the coach to be a mobile wreck. He had chosen a large area and limited its fuel for safety reasons. He had been expecting the steering to fail; which was why he would never take the bus onto the public road. He knew the brakes were useless. The vehicle however, was never completely out of control; he had had installed a dual braking system cunningly hidden and about which his students had never been aware.

As the bus trundled along ignominiously towards the Transport Depot, towed by the fire engine, the Padre explained all this to me. He also gave his assessment of my performance that afternoon. 'Fully believing we were heading into danger you overcame your natural instincts and did as I said without knowing whether I was right or wrong, and that showed faith.' I thought it showed stupidity but I thanked him for his compliment. We parted at the Control Tower, while the fire engine took the bus to the Transport Depot.

When I asked Peter Robinson what kind of Driving Lesson he had had to endure, he replied he had been led to believe an RAF transport aircraft with a faulty undercarriage was coming in to land with two hundred passengers on board. Only one wheel could be lowered. Peter had to drive the bus along the runway at fifty miles per hour in a dead straight line. Instead of saying he had never heard of anything so lunatic, Peter enquired if the roof of the bus would be strong enough to bear the weight of an aircraft. Padre Williams replied that he did not know because such a manoeuvre had never been practiced before, and in any case it was the only chance of survival facing the passengers. Peter was telling the Padre how sorry he felt for the passengers when the bus suddenly veered off the runway and started swerving all over the airfield when one of its own wheels fell off. He was just about to thank God the transport aircraft never arrived - when it did. Padre Williams, however, had made sure the bus was not on the runway at the time. Nor was there anything wrong with the aircraft.

The Driving Lesson planned for Robin Hilliard involved chasing after a light aircraft while it was taxiing towards the runway, to prevent it from taking off. The pilot was unaware the fuel gauge was stuck on the 'full' position, and was about to take off with insufficient fuel for his journey. They could not contact the pilot by radio because he was on a secret mission and radio silence orders were in force. Robin believed all this claptrap and accelerated along the perimeter track, caught up with the plane, but then found he could not slow down. The accelerator had indeed gone through the floorboards. He slammed on the brakes but they did not work. He swerved to the right to overtake it but the plane turned into the path of the bus. Robin swerved onto the grass to avoid the plane, straight into the path of a fire engine which was coming towards him across the runway. As he swerved to avoid this new danger, Padre Williams offered him a cigarette. Robin opened the door to jump from the bus. Padre Williams held him back, told him to relax, change into neutral and switch off the engine. The bus was approaching the runway. The aircraft was already on it. To Robin's amazement the bus slowed down and stopped before reaching the runway. The Padre had brakes of his own. The aircraft did not take off, it simply continued taxiing back whence it had come.

Padre Williams had been pleased with Peter's performance. He judged Peter had shown sympathy for those in peril in the air and had not flinched from the scatterbrained idea of using a wreck of an old bus for an airliner to balance on when coming in to land. In Robin's case, the Padre was pleased with his urgent sense of mercy in trying to prevent a pilot from taking off into danger, but his lack of faith in that he was about to jump from the bus left a lot to be desired. Padre Williams did say afterwards that he likened our driving of a bus with built-in faults to the pilot of an aircraft out of control who, the crew having bailed out, remains courageously at the controls to avoid a built-up area. The benefit we derived from these Driving Lessons often manifested itself in later years, for they had taught us how to react quickly in emergency situations. Padre Williams utilized teaching methods which were in advance of his time, for we learnt for ourselves through experience and we were able to act more quickly and decisively as a result.

Some months later, when, in his opinion presumably, we had sufficiently progressed along our respective 'exciting journeys on the road ahead through life', Padre Williams decided enough was enough. The old bus returned to the Scrap Yard, back into retirement. It had served its purpose well.

holly

Anthony spent many years in the RAF both home and abroad, continued serving the country as a Civil Servant in the Ministry of Defence and Meteorological Office, is now retired and living in the Forest of Dean. He has always been interested in writing - especially letters to the local Press.

I have been Chairman in the past, I've also been the Vice.
As Secretary too, I've been, it's all been rather nice.
There is one post which still I seek, for I'd like to be the measurer
Of all the Circle's treasure trove – one day I'll be the Treasurer.

John Stanley

A Forfeit for a Ribbon

From where she sat, on the curved cast-iron seat the council had
purchased when they had eventually decided to dignify the tump
with some landscaping, Dulcie could see the village street
unfolding from around the slope and drifting away down through
the cluster of cottages and scattering of shops, giving way to the
church at the bottom, by swinging right into the woods. Soon the
bell would be tolling its notice to the village worshippers that
attendance at the evening's service was now due. But for a few
more moments Dulcie could sit here and take advantage of the
Spring sunshine. She looked down at the small bunch of primroses
she held, the flowers collected from her garden where they grew
wild on the banks at the back. Their pale yellow faces picked up
the evening sun and down the petals of one of them, a tear
splashed into tiny droplets that glistened in the light. She thought
of her love for Alan Fletcher and always felt sorry she had never
paid the forfeit she owed him, though the game was long past
now.

* * *

The woods echoed with their laughter and teasing shouts as
it always had done. Since childhood, they had played their games
where the beech and oaks gave space for their running and
dodging and the bracken provided their spears and gave shelter for
the hiding. Now they were older, the trees gave privacy for their
games. Gangs were reduced to couples. Games drifted into
courting; the woods somewhere to wander out of view,
somewhere to play the teasing game with just the two of you, with
hesitant wishes – with hope.

Dulcie twisted her head away from the snatching fingers that
seemed intent on pulling the silky green ribbon from her pale-

yellow hair. 'Don'you dare, Alan Fletcher,' she said, side-stepping nimbly as he made yet another futile attempt to unravel the tempting band. Laughing, she skipped away through the trees, adding an edge of excited hysteria as she heard him running and whooping behind her.

Alan stopped and watched her run between the trunks, admiring the pale curls waving around the ribbon and the quick flashes of her petticoat and stockinged ankles as her skirt snagged on low-hanging branches. He smiled as she tugged herself free and set off again, then, silently, he stepped out of sight behind the thick trunk of an old oak and slid down into the stand of bracken alongside.

For a while he could hear only the soft sound of her laughter and then, a sudden hush in the forest. No longer could he detect the rustle of Dulcie's passage. Then, 'Alan?' He heard her call but kept very quiet. 'Alan? Where are you?' He made no answer. 'Alan! Have you gone home?' Her voice sounded nearer. 'ALAN!' the loud call seemed very close now. He heard the rustle of skirt against grass and suddenly there she was, not two paces away. He heard her mutter, 'Where has the silly goose got to?' And as she passed where he crouched, hidden in the green fronds, he rose, stepped forward and took hold of the green ribbon. One quick tug and the bow slid apart and the band slipped silkily through her hair, into his fingers.

She swung around, flushed with surprise. 'You cunning devil,' she said, her face developing a grin. 'Give it me back. That's not fair. Just typical of you, Alan Fletcher, to creep up on a person, behind her back. That's sneaky.'

'Sorry!' he said, holding the ribbon high. 'All's fair, so they say.'

She tried to jump up to catch it but Alan had the advantage of height and a way of waving the band just out of reach. Dulcie began to look annoyed.

'Our Mam'll be right mad if I d'come 'ome wi'out my

89

ribbon,' she said.

'Hmm!' Alan pretended to consider this new problem. 'Perhaps,' he said slowly, as though giving the solution great thought. 'Perhaps, the owner ought to pay something to retrieve it.'

'Like what?

'Hmm!' he thought a little more, then, 'How about paying a forfeit?'

'A forfeit? What kind of forfeit?'

'Well, for such a pretty object and one of clearly great value, I think …' he paused.

'You think what?'

'A kiss,' He stepped back holding his head to one side speculatively. 'Yes, 1 think it's definitely worth a kiss.'

'A kiss? You must be joking, Mr Fletcher. Who would want to kiss you? You're a big sneaky bully, creeping up on girls an' snachin' at them.'

'One little kiss; that's not much to ask for such a pretty ribbon.' Dulcie looked at him with a small frown, as though considering the request.

'Only one kiss, and then you'll give the ribbon back?'

'Gentleman's word.'

'But it's not proper to kiss a feller alone in the wood and anyway I be shy. I don' think I could do it proper with you lookin.'

'I 'spose you want me t'close my eyes, an then you'll run away.'

'Don' be daft; you'll still have the ribbon.'

'So what then.'

Dulcie thought for a moment and then, 'I know what's fair. You shut your eyes and count to thirty, slowly mind, and I'll kiss you durin.'

'On the lips.'

'On the cheek, you cheeky devil.'

'All right - and what about the ribbon?'

Dulcie pretended to ponder as though she had forgotten all about the ribbon. 'Oh!' she said. 'Just hang it round yer collar. I'll trust you to give it me after I kissed you.' Alan smiled and draped the silky green band over his shoulders, smoothing it down against his shirt. 'Right,' he said and closed his eyes.

'Start counting, slowly mind, up to thirty.' Dulcie ordered.

'One, two, three, four,' Alan silently counted the seconds away, listening for unusual sounds: hoping to feel the soft brush of his sweetheart's breath against his cheek as she approached. There was silence around the counting and he began to worry, was she still there, was she coming closer, could he move his lips in time to meet hers? He reached to sixteen and suddenly could stand the suspense no longer. He opened his eyes. Dulcie stood directly in front of him, leaning forward, lips poised in the form of a kiss.

'I knew I couldn't trust thee, Alan Fletcher,' she said scornfully, stepping back a pace. 'You be just a darn ordinary cheatin' feller; now give me back my ribbon.'

'Oh, come on Dulcie,' Alan looked sorrowful at the lass. 'Give I another chance. Go on, just one more. I promise faithful I won't cheat this time.'

'You'd better not, Alan Fletcher, or I'll never speak to thee again.' said Dulcie admonishingly. Alan smiled, satisfied and closed his eyes again, tighter this time, determined not to lose the chance of feeling Dulcie's lips caress his cheek, or even his lips, if he could judge it right. She couldn't object once it happened. He started to count. Above the sound of his voice it was as quiet as before. His senses sharpened; he thought he could feel her close; there seemed to be a whisper of movement, a slight sense of nearness. He counted on, passed twenty, fought the urge to squint through one eye, until suddenly he found himself saying, '... twenty-nine, thirty.' He opened his eyes.

All he saw were trees. He spun quickly around looking

hopefully in all directions but only saw trees and bracken and grass. Dulcie had vanished. He shook his head; it was incredulous that his girl could have played such a trick on him. Him, Alan Fletcher, taken in by a lass. It was unbelievable. Suddenly he remembered, all was not lost; at least he still had the ribbon. His hands dabbed at his front, seeking the reassurance of a silken touch. His face fell in dismay as his fingers met only the coarse cotton of his shirt. Alan felt suddenly deflated, she had taken not only his prize but also his pride along with it.

But as he made his way out of the forest, a new pride developed in its place, one that grew from the realisation that he had a girl to be proud of, a girl like no other, a sharp, clever lass and one well worth the courting. And in the future there would come a time when he would be ready to reclaim his forfeit and she would be most glad to pay it.

This is an extract from a much longer story called 'A Forfeit of Feathers' which is set during World War One.

BODY LANGUAGE

Grandfather Braggs couldn't believe his luck. Across the room Martha Beadle had winked at him. In order to disguise a too obvious interest, he dabbed a finger, in what he intended to be a nonchalant gesture, into the bowl of his pipe, tamping down the freshly lit tobacco – then rapidly removed it, trying in vain to shake off the red-hot shreds that clung to his burning skin. Pressing his fingers hard between his crossed knees, he groaned and squeaked through teeth clamped tight in an effort to muffle the sounds.

Martha Beadle removed her hanky from her sleeve and dabbing away at the dust that had caused her eye to twitch, wiped away the irritation. Her attention was caught by the strange antics of old Sidney Braggs who was sitting near the door. The silly old devil was squirming about in his seat, hissing like some dissertating serpent and scattering smouldering shreds of tobacco about the place. One day, she thought, he'll burn the whole building down, the stupid old goat. She had never been able to come to terms with tobacco, nor with those that used it. She found it dirty and disgusting; all that ash drifting down one's front and the deep brown stains coating fingers and moustache, whilst the smell – well! Her lips drew back in a snarl of distaste as she contemplated the reek of stale tobacco smoke that must be emanating from Braggs's old pullover.

Good heavens, thought Sidney, she's smiling at me now. He glanced around the Day Room to see if any of the other residents had noticed his good fortune but on his side of the room the men were all hunched in slumber and quite oblivious to matters carnal. They squatted in a row against the wall of windows, baking in the sunlight like cacti on a shelf, wrinkled, dry and potentially prickly. On Martha's side, the other ladies in the line were too engrossed in mumbled gossip, their close nodding heads preventing them from noticing anything beyond their neighbour. Quite deliberately therefore, Sidney smiled at Martha and followed up with a sly wink. She shouldn't miss that, he thought.

Now Martha was noted for her temper. It was so often bad and she kept it on a short fuse, so was liable to explode at any instant. What is more, nothing moved her to detonate more quickly than the inane behaviour of her peers. Thus she felt her anger increasing beyond mere irritation as she watched the ridiculous antics of Sidney Braggs. Just look at the old fool, she thought, sitting there grinning and twitching, he can't be all there.

Angrily, she tugged at her cuffs and skirt, venting her temper on her clothing.

Sidney sighed at the signs. They definitely confirmed his suspicions – she was aware of him alright. That was quite evident in the coy manner displayed whilst brushing her sleeves and in the provocative – dare he say it – seductive way she had of smoothing her skirt. She was most certainly flirting with him. Thus emboldened, his eyes strayed to her legs. There was little to see beneath the wrinkled lisle but with a little imagination – well, Sidney blushed.

Martha exploded within. The dirty old devil – he's looking up my skirts. The nerve of the man. No wonder his cheeks are flushed; sweating with embarrassment I dare say. And I should darn well think so too, the impudent – pervert. Well, I'm not standing for this. I'm going up to my room before I lose my rag completely. She pulled herself out of her chair and taking up the walking-stick propped close to hand, hobbled slowly and arthritically across the room towards the door.

Oh my God, she's coming over, gasped Sidney, whatever shall I say? Martha was proving to be a lot more forward than one had a right to expect from a lady of her mature years. A mild flirtation across the strip of Wilton was one thing, but close encounters of the romantic kind were more than he was ready for, no matter how much encouraged – besides, this was hardly the place. However, never one to shy impotently from a lady's approach, Sidney rose painfully to his feet and leaned, in what he hoped was a casual manner, against the frame of his Zimmer. Not having a hat to doff, he could only nod his head – but gallantly.

Martha saw red. How much more could a soul take? Now the old duffer was deliberately blocking her path, standing in front of the door, leaning on that contraption and shaking his head like a madman. She stopped in front of him, flushed purple with anger and shaking with rage.

My goodness, she's pretty when she blushes, thought Sidney, and she trembles so much. It must be our closeness that arouses her. It was clear that his technique was still formidable for it was obvious that Martha had developed a desperate need for him. Realising how much she wanted him, Sidney's excitement rose to new and glorious heights - as did his blood pressure.

Beyond control now, Martha raised her stick to strike at the stupid clown dithering and doddering in front of her, but the action threw her off-balance and she put out her hand to clutch at the walking-frame, to steady herself - and touched Sidney's hand instead.

Oh bliss, cried Sidney, grasping her arthritic fingers in his, she's wild about me. Waves of romantic passion swept through him; desire thrashed at his body; lust lashed out at his heartstrings so that his blood flowed wildly, without direction. Suddenly, confused chambers failed to accept the extra demands imposed by Sidney's ardour and so burst apart. Not knowing his heart was broken, only recognizing a great rush of passion, Sidney drowned in his love for Martha. He fell to the floor dragging the Zimmer, and Martha's only support, with him. They sprawled together on the carpet, Martha, writhing in despair, straddling Sidney's already immobile body.

Oh blast it to hell, I can't move, Martha cried in despair, trying to get a grip on Sidney's shirt to push herself up. But she only succeeded in collapsing once more onto his stricken body. Oh damn the man, she groaned, what is he playing at now? How dreadfully embarrassing in front of all these stupid gawpers.

Desperately she pleaded, won't someone lift me off this idiot? - but no-one seemed to hear her.

What a way I have with the ladies, mused Sidney, drifting away as the pain eased. It's often been my downfall - though I remember no encounter so passionate as this. If only I didn't feel so tired. He groaned regrettably as he felt Martha moving sensuously over his body, her hot fingers ripping desperately at his clothing. Not now dear, he said. Maybe tomorrow, that will be something to look forward to, smiling at the thought, as he quietly passed away.

oak

John is a retired school teacher. A founder member of the Circle, he once held the Chair and now holds the post of treasurer. He is also the Circle's reporter. He compiled and edited Forest Leaves Two. At home, pride of place is given to the cup awarded at the Stroud Festival for his Armada play. He is mainly recognized as a writer of short stories and occasional verse.

Joanna Trevor

WAGES OF SIN

(a working title)

Chapter 1

'The wages of sin is death!'
His voice rang out in the lovely Wren church. All eyes were fixed on his austere, finely drawn face, all had his attention. The Reverend Richard Reece looked around him benignly, almost lovingly, letting his gaze move from one to another.

His voice dropped a level, so that they had to strain a little to hear him.

'...but the gift of God is eternal through Christ Jesus our Lord.'

In a more conversational tone he said, 'Did you think that sin itself was dead? That this *evil and adulterous generation* was immune to the wages of sin?'

He raised then lowered his elegant shoulders, as if to shrug off such pernicious thought. His voice rose again theatrically as he continued:

'We live in a degenerate age which, with all its technological advances, with all its opportunities to render good in the world, rather, turns everything to the service of Satan. And do not doubt that he exists; he is alive and thriving in the world now. And we serve him who do not recognise his innumerable temptations.'

Most of his audience consisted of young people. They ought perhaps to have found his pronouncements archaic and alien, yet he seemed to make them real, vital and urgent. Perhaps the very urbanity of the man, his forceful delivery, his personal attractiveness, made his ideas as compelling as his manner.

The lights glinted on his silver grey hair as he turned his head and made eye contact with each person seated before him, and each lowered their eyes and even their heads before his penetrating gaze.

They were in groups, their seats arranged in a semi-circle, facing him. The Reverend Reece now descended the stone steps and rested his back against the carved surface of the pulpit as he stood and let his eyes continue to move over the assembly. He still towered above them, well over six foot tall and elegant in his priest's uniform.

They heard a sigh come from his lips. 'But, *all manner of sins shall be forgiven.*'

He smiled for the first time, his body taking a more relaxed pose.

'That is why you are all here, on the Omega Course: to save yourselves from the consequences of sin and to begin your lives anew. We all know that we are at the time of the End of Days, and that the coming judgement is a reality.'

Another, unseen pair of eyes watched him, hidden in the dim light behind a pillar in the south transept. These eyes were cold, the mouth a thin line, the face otherwise expressionless. There was nothing there of the warm attention and admiration of the other faces in the church.

Reece took a chair and sat casually, his arms leaning on its back.

'Don't imagine that sin *has* somehow gone out of fashion, or that in our *laissez faire* age it no longer exists. It is thriving, more than ever. And the responsibility of you all is to search your hearts, your *souls*, and weed out the corruption that is lying there. And strive to be free of Satan in your lives, for he is cunning and comes in many disguises. If you value your eternal souls then you will cleave to the teachings of this course and so guarantee your eternal salvation.'

He stood and replaced the chair, smiling gently on them.

'Some of you have been here before, some of you are new to us. Welcome all.' He looked around the groups to individuals who were stirring in readiness for his command.

'My helpers will assist in forming your circles and beginning your work for this evening. The quotation for discussion this time from Isiah 30 verse 1, is: *Woe to the rebellious children, saith the Lord, that take counsel, but not of me, that cover with a covering, but not of my spirit, that they may add to sin.'*

There was a scraping of chair legs as the groups reorganised themselves, shepherded by young men dressed in black jeans and black tee shirts. The Reverend Richard Reece strode off to the right, the skirts of his cassock flapping about his long legs.

Someone waited close by and hidden from members of the course, a tall young woman with short dark hair, her shining face turned towards him in welcome.

'You were wonderful, as usual,' she said, 'I believe you mesmerise them.'

'Heaven forfend,' Richard Reece said piously, though his eyes shone in response to hers and she could tell he was pleased.

'Indeed!' she replied, with a quick grin. 'We can't have any inappropriate hero worship in the House of God. "No other God before me" and all that. But what are you to do? Who could be immune to your charisma,' she added lightly. 'Or, indeed, to your great beauty,' she said more softly, reaching to stroke his cheek with the back of her hand.

He clasped it and held it where it was for a moment, then dropped it to the level of his elaborate crucifix and held it between them, their bodies drawn closer together. They were standing in the centre of the south transept close by the nave, the light much dimmer than where the groups of sinners were now earnestly discussing their lives' failings.

'Any news from your parents?' he asked now, releasing her hand and fondling his crucifix.

'Yes. It's all fixed. We're going there this weekend.' Alicia searched his face anxiously. 'You did say you were free then?'

He nodded. 'Did you tell them what it was about?'

'That I am to be married, yes. They are delighted.'

'To me?' he queried, and lifted his head a little so that he looked down his finely moulded nose at her.

'I just said your name: Richard. I thought there would be plenty of time for them to know who and what you are when we get there.'

'You felt that the fact that I am a priest might prejudice them in advance?' He raised an eyebrow at her making the question seem less edged. She laughed and placed her hands on either side of his face.

'Hardly! I suspect that they will be very impressed and delighted that their errant daughter has at last chosen the true path with a man of impeccable morals – and even some fame.' Admiration lit her eyes.

He put his hands over hers. 'And you explained that we shall have separate beds? No assumptions to be made on the basis of your *errant* past.'

'Yes, yes. As ever, until our wedding night. There are enough bedrooms to choose from anyway. It's a quiet time, coming up to Easter.'

They fell silent for a moment, eyes on each other's faces. The low murmur of voices could be heard coming from the nave and, incongruously, a sudden crack of laughter.

'There is something else,' she added. 'My mother was so excited about our engagement she rang me back and said she had invited a friend of mine. To make it more of a celebration.' She was aware of the defensiveness in her voice. Perhaps she should have sounded more assertive, she thought, as she saw him frown.

'Male or female?' he asked, his voice non-committal.

'A woman. An old friend.'

'But not old, I hope. Is she pretty?' He was looking more

compliant.

'No,' Alicia said. As his face fell she added, smiling, 'She's beautiful.'

'Well that's all right then.' The Reverend Reece gave a low laugh and placed an arm around her shoulders, leading her to the vestry door.

hawthorn

Joanna is a well-published author having had six books published in the series featuring Detective Christopher Simon and his partner Jessie Thurrow. She is currently working on the next book in the series, of which the above is an extract.

Her first two books, 'A Gathering of Dust' and 'The Same Corruption There' were published by Piatkus. 'A Time to Die', 'A Fine and Private Place', 'A Deadly Deceit' and 'Murder in the Cathedral Clinic' are published by Hale. All her books are available in large print.

Sean Walsh

Stepping the Mast

Joachim and Matthias were standing by the dockside. After her trouble-free launch the 'Marieke' was being fitted out. In the bright, warm sunshine the pristine hull lay moored in one of the basins of the Binnehafen at Emsmünde while teams of shipwrights sweated to make ready for her maiden voyage. It seemed that recent setbacks had been forgotten. The ever-ready Baumeister, whom everyone had heard of but hardly anyone knew, acted mostly through a seemingly endless procession of clerks and agents, promising a bonus for the shipwrights if they completed the vessel ahead of schedule.

'I didn't think they'd ever get it built,' said Joachim, 'not with all the fighting that was going on. Did you see them at the Town Hall? All the men – the shipwrights – were banging on the doors and shouting. It looked as if they were going to break the door down. Then one of the merchants came out and tried to talk to them. They weren't in the mood to listen; he beat a hasty retreat inside. I thought they were going to lynch him!'

'Do you know what the problem was?'

'They ran out of money, I think. I spoke to my father about it and he said these things happen when you invest in a ship. Sometimes it doesn't get built at all. Sometimes it lies half-built for months, years even, till someone puts up the money to finish it. Or it gets built, and then sinks on its maiden voyage – you end up losing everything.'

'That's just about the worst thing that can happen. And I've heard sailors say that if a ship loses a man on her maiden voyage, it means she's blighted and no one will sail on her. Ships have been broken up because of that.' They watched as the men began fitting the mainmast using a crane known as a 'sheer-legs'. This was a sort of derrick which straddled the deck, from which the mainmast was lowered into its seating in the bottom of the ship.

This had to be done with extreme care, inching the heavy mast downward little by little until it rested on its base and could be secured. The main danger with this operation was that the lifting tackle might fail, causing the mast to plunge through the ship's bottom. They watched for a long time as the shipwrights continued with the delicate task. They had guided the bottom end of the mast through its recess in the waist. Unseen, below decks, more groups of men were ready to guide it as it descended through each recess. Suddenly they saw that the sheer-legs were about to give way! Something was wrong with the lifting-tackle!

There was an unhealthy, ominous creaking sound and the derrick began to shake and judder - Matthias shouted a warning, then the men on deck realised the danger and shouted in turn frantically to their comrades below. At that moment the tackle gave way and the mast plunged into the belly of the ship with a resounding BOOM! The report echoed back off the quayside and the walls of the adjoining houses. For a few moments the men on deck stood in disbelief, then as one they rushed below, and promptly ran into more men hurrying up on deck. For a few minutes there was complete confusion.

Eventually they managed to get back into some sort of order. The yard foreman, who had now taken charge again, sent a few men below to check whether there were any injured, if the ship was taking on water and if so, how badly. There were a few slight injuries, mostly caused by rope burns, but the damage to the hull was more serious. The mast had struck the seating, bounced off and cracked the timbers.

'Ohgodalmighty, she's sprung a leak,' said a voice, with an air of desperation. Every able-bodied man who could be spared now faced a frantic, dangerous race against time. The shout went up and the ship's bell rang wildly, to be joined by others at the dockside. Tradesmen downed their tools and rushed from all sides to help, more dashed out from the nearby taverns and houses, all rivalries and animosities forgotten. Buckets, pails, pots, bowls, anything which could hold water was pressed into service, as a chain was formed through the ship from bilges to gunwale to bail the water out. It was as yet little more than a trickle, but the action of the water against the weakened timber meant that the leak would almost certainly worsen if not stopped as soon as possible. Unless they acted quickly, the ship would be doomed. Yet more men, sailors and stevedores, manoeuvred lighters into position and set up lines to tow the 'Marieke' to the nearest dry dock, while those assigned to bailing frantically scooped and carried and the carpenters struggled to make some temporary repair. Within a few hours the vessel had been brought to the dry dock. So, the maiden voyage was going to be delayed again. Another costly operation! Was there no end to the trials of building this ship?

The shipwrights began to murmur and mutter, fearing another stoppage due to lack of money but there was nothing they could do but carry on with their work. Meanwhile, another conference of the merchants had to be hastily summoned. For everyone with a stake in the ship, it meant more hustle and bustle, anxiety and misgivings and wanting someone to blame. The upshot of all this was more grief for the shipbuilders' chief clerk, who had only just recovered from the last fiasco. Again it seemed as if everyone was after his blood. The merchants sought to blame him if the ship did not get built, while the shipwrights wanted to blame him for what they saw as the failures of the consortium.

Heated debate ebbed and flowed across the table, like the sea itself …'Oh, for Christ's sake! Is there no end to these troubles?'

'Who in hell's name let the tackle slip? Didn't we pay for good ropes?' The damage was greater than at first thought, with several timbers needing replacement. With the ship laid up in dry dock after this unforeseen setback, at least another fifth was estimated to be added to the original cost of construction. It seemed that the chance of profits in a trading ship for many people was rapidly disappearing ... The better-organised shipwrights now sent a deputation from their Guild. They had started listing their demands and were trying to negotiate.

'We want our wages paid in advance ...'

'What?'

Baumeister, was none too pleased when he realised the predicament. 'HOW much will it cost to keep the ship in dry dock? What is it about you people, that you think because I brew beer that I am made of money?'

'At this rate, the ship will never get built. All the money sunk into this venture will be lost. How can it be that so many things can go wrong?'

'... when you invest in a ship you take a risk. That is the nature of business venture. You cannot avoid I ...'

Joachim and the others could only guess at what the adults meant when they spoke of trade, for they revealed little to their children. They told mostly fairy-tales, about sea-monsters and far away places. Once he had seen a book containing pictures of strange creatures, which were supposed to inhabit the far-off lands being discovered by the explorers. A mystery they were, and a mystery they would remain, for all that his elders would tell him.

This is an extract from 'The Shipbuilders' Almanack', a novel in progress set in 16th century Germany.

beech

Sean has been a member of the Dean Writers' Circle since moving to the Forest in 2004. His varied interests include industrial archaeology, conservation and web design. He looks after the Circle's web site.

David Warren

- The Entity

The Entity

The three young men sat on the Dock wall discussing stars and planets when a deafening roar echoed up the bay. Stumbling to their feet, they watched a ball of light smash into the field near to where they stood. Running to where the object lay, they stood at the fence, the heat making them sweat. There was movement.

My name is Quinten. I teach science at a secondary school and on Wednesdays I run an after school class, a bit of fun for the kids, based on the unexplained. We talk about ghosts, UFO's, Nessie and many other anomalies.

Wednesday arrived as usual and in walked my after school class, four girls and three boys. They sat as far apart as possible and I turned towards the whiteboard and wrote "Aliens".

'Now who could explain this to me? What are Aliens?' I asked.

A few shouts came my way of little green men and grays from the girls but the three lads said nothing; they just stared at the table. I finished writing the spider gram on the board and then set the next task of drawing aliens. I took a slow walk over and stopped at the girls' table. I had a bit of a laugh at the furry ET that had been drawn.

After the giggles had stopped, my eyes drifted to the lads on the other table. They were huddled together but I could hear parts of conversation. It was something about food, meeting after school and the body.

Now being a teacher I've overheard many a story of girls next door and on the tele, so I took it they were talking about some young women they had spotted. As I got closer the muffled voices abruptly stopped. Xzavier started to draw on the paper. I peered over his shoulder and he was scribbling a drawing of a Dalek.

I pulled a stool over and jokingly said, 'Who is this new lovely lady in your lives then?'

I had asked hoping for a laugh; instead they just sat there looking at me, all of them looking tired and pale. I quickly changed the subject, talking about last month's UFO magazine until Zander spoke.

'Sir!' he said. 'Could we have a chat at the end of the lesson?'

The time shot by as usual and soon it was the end of the lesson. I was stacking the books I had to mark. The girls had left and the boys edged their way towards me.

'What's up?' I asked, not taking my eyes off the minutes of last week's parents meeting.

'Sir, could you meet us tonight at the Docks? It's important. We need to show you something. Please come - at eight.' They dashed for the door, shouted 'See you!' and were gone.

The drive home took longer than usual. Being autumn, the wind had picked up and the smell of clean, fresh fish rolled off the Docks. The cars in front seemed not to understand that 30 mph meant 30 not 10.

I pulled up outside my box-flat and lifted the books from the back seat. Struggling to type in the code, the door was ripped out of reach. There stood a woman, young looking, near my age, pretty, with long red hair.

'Hello!' I said.

'Your neighbour let me in.' she said. 'I'm Xzavier's mother.'

'Hi!' I stuttered. We climbed the stairs and, after giving the door the boot, we walked in and were quickly attacked by Murr the cat. I flicked the kettle on and returned to the living-room. I sat in the recliner opposite her.

'How can I help you,' I said. With tears streaming down her face she looked at me. My heart sank but I tried to look concerned as she told me her story. The thing that took me out of my trance was the kettle switching itself off. I left Mrs. Smith sobbing into her hanky. I poured the coffee and ran the story she had just told over in my head. Xzavier was stealing from her, she was saying about drugs and what he owes, when his father died and they were left with nothing.

This woman that sat before me had a lot of troubles, lived hard and looked after Xzavier with all her heart but now this. But she was beautiful, her long shapely legs, her watery eyes, her breasts hidden behind a high-neck top. I tried to comfort her and told her we would meet again, 'after tonight when I meet the boys'.

She left and my heart was aching. I had never met his mother before. Every parent evening had been attended by his grandmother. Mrs. Smith was beautiful and I was infuriated with myself for being so ignorant about my pupil's family. I lay on the couch and munched some toast, watching the news about the meteor that crashed in a local field, watching the clock on the video tick by. I went for a shower and tried to relax, thinking about what I was going to say to Xzavier

The trip to the docks took longer than ever with my head thinking about the lady that had entered my life and the thoughts were of her holding my hand in the wood. I turned left and my car struggled over the rocky ground.

At the first turning I pulled in. Slipping on my coat I realized the wind had picked up and was causing the car to rock. I slipped out into the night walking towards the end of the pier.

'Sir!' came a voice from the hedge.

'Hello!' I said.

'There is a gap in the hedge just down there. Come up to the barn.' Pulling one door across I slid in. The place was badly lit with torches. The boys were all sat on hay bales. I walked towards them.

'Stop!' Xzavier said, standing up.

'Hey!' I said.

'Stand still sir,' came the reply.'
I stopped and looked at them. Xzavier walked closer to me.

'Now Sir, please don't panic. Do you know that meteorite that crashed the other night Well, we found it and it was not a meteorite.'

'What?' I said.

'Sir, let us finish with that.'

A beautiful young woman walked out from behind some tall stacks of hay. She looked at me, then I heard the voice in my head. 'Hello sir, please do not panic.'

With this there was a rush of wind and I was in a city, a very futuristic city. There were screams and smashes coming from all directions. Then I looked to the skies. There were two moons and one was massive. I looked down.

There were people rushing every where; people lay bleeding in the street. I tried to shelter my eyes from the children that lay there dying. I wanted to run away to escape but I was rooted to the spot. I stood there, my hands over my eyes praying that it would end. I started to fall, then I opened my eyes.

Xzavier was looking over. 'Sir, you ok?'

'Where am I?'

Pulling myself up, I tried to get to my feet but the world spun. What had happened? There were bodies all over, screaming children. I felt a hand rest on my shoulder.

'That was Arwin's home planet. It was destroyed by a moon that was knocked out of orbit by a comet. We have all seen it, Sir. Arwin and her family and many others are wandering the solar system looking for a new home. They were going to choose here but they say we are not ready to accept them yet. They are coming to get Arwin tonight. We have to get her to the highest place but the government knows she is here and are hunting her down.'

With this, the door burst open. In ran Xzavier's mother. She got within a couple of feet of Xzavier and then lay on the floor crying. I realized that she was now seeing what I had just witnessed. We sat there silent, waiting for her to come round. I had rested her head upon my lap.

'Help!' came a whisper. A few minutes later, 'Please help.'

I lifted her head and her eyes blinked open. She tried to jump up but like me her legs had failed.

'Mum, this is Arwin. She is sorry. What you just saw was her home being destroyed by a comet. Please help us. We need to get her to the top of Foxes Run tonight.'

The plan was made. First the boys would go the long way and draw the attention of anyone that was watching. Then we would leave the dark way across the fields where we could get to Xzavier's mother's car, which we could then take to the bottom of Foxes Run. Then would come the long trek to the top.

And so it began. We outed our torches and the boys, though worried, left, making as much noise as they could. I could hear them singing. Then the lights came on and the cars turned to them and they started running. Then we left. The field had been ploughed, so moving quickly was a no-go.

We made good across the field and we could see the car hidden amongst a small group of trees. Then I heard a sound, then lights and soon after a chopper passed right over us. It turned almost instantly. We ran.

Arwin made good progress over the ground but Xzavier's mother held my hand tight to try to stop herself from falling. The helicopter was now blinding us with its light. We had stopped before I had known it.

'Do not try to run!' came a voice from the light. We are armed and are willing to fire on you if you try to resist.'

At this Arwin waved her hand. Then there was a scream. The man and the pilot were holding their heads. They were now seeing what we had seen. She grabbed my free hand and started to run. We ran with her and the car was now in reach. We clambered in and the car pulled off with ease and we were on are way to the mount.

The drive was easy but I had to keep checking the mirror to see if we were being followed – nothing. I looked at Arwin in the mirror.

'I did not hurt them.' she said. I smiled, the thought of this being a dream still playing in my head. The houses started to thin and were replaced by tall oak trees, then the ground started to rise. Another mile, then we had to leave the car, but it approached us quicker than I thought. We sat in the car waiting for what I still don't know. We were meeting the boys on the ridge where we hoped Arwin would be picked up.

We climbed out of the car and took to the path. It rose steeply to the left and I knew the ridge would be only a half mile more. The sound hit us straight away. There were cars coming and lots of them. We sped along, my legs were aching from the up-hill climb, but I persisted, still holding Xzavier's mother's hand. I pulled to my speed. She never complained but just walked with us. I saw a flash in the distance and turned quickly behind to see how much time we had. I sent the flash back. It was the boys. They had made it.

We came in to the open and Arwin knelt down. There was a shrill sound and everything went silent. It was like being deaf. The wind had turned itself off. Then came the lights, the sky lit up like it was on fire, then there was a droning sound and a ship appeared in the sky. Xzavier looked at me.

'I want to go with Arwin.' he said. 'I don't want to be here. Please let me go, Mum.' he said, turning his head to face her. Tears were streaming down her face and I pulled her near. He turned back to me and grabbed my free hand.

'Look after her. I will come back when I've learned to drive.' he said, with a smile, then ran towards Arwin. He held her hand and looked over.

I felt a movement next to me as his mother tried to make a run but I held her tight and her face was in my shoulder crying again. I turned to see a hundred torches running towards us. As I turned there was a flash of light and they were gone. I sank to my knees exhaustion taking over me and listening to the sobs on my shoulder.

It's been five years since we saw Xzavier last and as you can guess me and Kristin Smith are to be married. After all the tests the scientists did on us we fell deeply in love. It's a week until the wedding and I have left an invite on top of the Foxes Hill. I just hope he passed his test in time.

David, one of our younger members, was brought up in Ireland but now lives in the Forest of Dean. He has been a member of the Circle for a good number of years and has held positions of Vice-Chairman and Chairman. He is dyslexic but in his own words says, '- with a burning ambition to write, I will not be beaten by my dyslexia. I will write until the words turn right.'

Toni Wilde

GENIE

I am a Genie
in a bottle
CORKED
don't pull
the cork
you'll let
me out and
I'll scream
LOUDLY
touch the glass gently
don't tap it touch the glass
gently it will ring in my ears
reverberate as sound waves again
and again repeating until muffled
by the cork it dies I've got used to it
being in here I quite like it really the
world outside looks foggy it must be
my breath clouding the glass I can't
see you or you or you clearly you all
look like ghosts I can't hear your
voices mouthing words that don't
make sense I think you'd like to
let me out all hell break loose
or just a whimper a puff of
wind and I'm gone.

Ladies Night

That happy crowd – the regular swimmers on Ladies Night, laughing and joking in the changing room – a new costume here, weight loss there and – just look at that tan. Where did you get that? Morocco? No – a sunbed.

To the pool, padding along in single file – overhead cold shower – underfoot – foot-bath – Ugh – the worst bit. Into the water, some gingerly down the steps - experiencing cold creeping up the costume.

Anna dives in, soon gets into her stride, powering up the pool, skirts round the huddle gossiping in the middle, carves between two friends coming the other way, cuts in front of a width swimmer, touches the wall and back again, all set for her fifty lengths. She establishes an easy breast stroke, blue costume overtaking yellow, finding a line.

Ten lengths, twenty, the numbers are thinning out, some in the sauna, some off home. The rhythm of her strokes, breathing out as she pushes back, in as she cuts the water forward, clears her head, brushes the cobwebs away. The gentle repetitive movement brings waves of thoughts, first memories of swimming baths – intense cold – shivering – blue flesh – white, numb fingers and toes – her father trying to teach her, the exhilaration of swimming back-stroke beside him, safe on the inside nearest the wall, the arched ceiling of the tiled Victorian emporium, ornate ironwork, wooden half-doors of the changing booths lining the pool sides, the balcony above, cubicles where people bathed who had no domestic baths at home. She remembers the noises echoing, the ceiling lit by glass bricks.

Thirty lengths - not many in the pool now. Clear water ahead and to the side of her. She glances left to where the three life-guards, one male and two female are deep in conversation. Thinks – they wouldn't notice if I started drowning. Destroys her rhythm – takes in water – choking, makes it to the deep end, pauses to recover, looks around. A girl in pink, long dark hair flowing behind her, swims up, doggy paddle, reaches the wall, relieved, stays there while Anna sets off again.

Fifteen to go; swims past a bright pink costume going the other way once, twice; third time, misses her – thinks colours – tan shoes and pink shoe laces – party frocks, frills – Wendy, her best friend in junior school, five frills on her pink dress – hers yellow, with only two frills – pink ribbons round Wendy's dark ringlets tied in rags at night, remembers begging her own mother to do the same with hers.

Near the deep end, a vision of pink swirling below – taffeta she wonders? Arms and legs – she reaches the wall, turns, pushes off, surfaces, sees ahead the girl in the pink costume, panicking, arms flailing, trying to cry out – no sound. The life-guards seem to be sharing a joke, one of them back turned to the pool, the other two laughing. Can't they see? She shouts but they don't hear. She looks around the pool. There is no-one else in the water – only her. She swims towards the girl as she disappears beneath the surface, reaches where she saw her last – no sign; dives below – the water seems murky. It feels like ribbons of sea-weed wrapping round her legs. She searches round and round – no trace. Up for air twice – tries to attract the attention of the life-guards, still laughing – scans the surface for a glimpse of pink – nothing. Again she dives, searches – nothing, and again. Terror mounting, it must be several minutes – could she survive? She visualises the long dark hair - seems to see it floating on the surface and imagines turning the girl face upwards. The face looks like Wendy, so pretty, so grey, so dead.

One of the life-guards steps forward, calls, 'Time please.' Anna swims over. 'There's a girl over there - in a pink costume - I saw her go under - I can't find her.'

The life-guard blows her whistle. All three come to the edge of the pool, scanning the water.

'You come out dear.' She says to Anna. On the side Anna scans the water, still choppy, wide expanse of blue. Where is she?

'There's no-one there, dear. She must have got out. You go and get changed. Probably see her in the changing room.'

Anna takes a long last survey of the pool before going into the communal changing room where a few women are drying themselves. She stands watching them for a moment, recognising some, but not the girl with the long dark hair.

Under the shower, shampoo fluffing through her fingers, bubbles coursing down her legs, the scent thick in her nostrils, she sees the girl behind closed eyelids, the panic in her face, the unheard screams, the desperate bid for help. She sees her clearly. Could it be - Wendy?

And then she remembers. When she was eight, Wendy's parents moved house and she went to a different school. At ten she hit the headlines. She and an older boy had gone to some old quarry workings. The area was fenced off, prohibited to the public. It was a favourite haunt of children who had breached the wire in several places. According to the media, they were playing on a gravel slope above the water-filled pit when she slipped and fell in the water. The boy had jumped in after her, dived repeatedly trying to find her. When her body was recovered, her legs had been entangled in metal bands - like ribbons of sea-weed - thinks Anna.

She returns to the changing room to dry and dress herself. Bending down, drying between her toes, she touches a wet pink costume on the floor. She looks up at a girl drying her long dark hair with a white towel

'Are you all right?' she asks.

'Yes, thank you.'

'I saw you in the pool - in the deep end. You were panicking. 1 tried to help.'

'Me - in the deep end? 1 don't think so. 1 can't swim. I've been in the sauna. It must have been some-one else.'

'Yes.' Says Anna. She's sure now - a ghost from the past.

Bolt for Freedom

It's been a long night. I'm worried about Al. He's so hyper. He didn't come home till 6am. He woke me up – I'd only just dropped off. I could have killed him. It was such a relief to see him. Then I was cross.

-Where have you been? I said. – I was worried about you.

-So? he said – I don't have to answer to you for everything I do. I don't even live here.

-You do at the moment. I said. – You should tell me when you're going to be late. What would your parents say if they knew you were out all night?

-They wouldn't care. They're not like you – always fussing. They trust me.

-I doubt that. I said.

It just slipped out. I could have kicked myself. I saw his expression change. His hand touched the lock on the front door. He was gone before I could stop him. I shouted after him.
- Al! Al!
-

Al turns the corner, stops under the lamp-post. It's not yet daylight and the lamp is still on. It casts a yellow stain on the wet pavement. He leans against the post, knocking his hip on the waste bin. It is overflowing – chip papers and cans, MacDonald's leftovers. It turns his stomach. He's breathing heavy. He hates Julie. You wouldn't think his Mum and her were sisters. She's nothing like his Mum. He can hear her calling
- Al, Al!
He starts to run.

I've rung the police. What else could I do? He's been missing all day. They say it's not unusual for boys of his age to take time out after a row. Time out! What does that mean? Crazy psycho-speak if you ask me. They told me to ring again if he's not back before midnight. I'm sick with worry.

7-30pm. Not yet dark. I won't phone Elaine just yet. Wait till 8 o'clock. It will be dark then. If he's not back, I'll ring her. If I was his Mum, I'd want to know – I'd want to know now – but it might be a false alarm. The police deal with runaway children all the time, don't they? They said he'll probably come home once it gets dark.

Al is hungry. He's a healthy growing boy. He's spent all the cash he had in his pockets. He stands in the doorway of Marks and Spencers with his hand out.
- Can you spare any change, Mister?
-Bugger off!

And
- Clear off Kid. This is my patch! A piece of advice – Go home, this is no place for a kid like you.

He tries the railway station. He approaches a well-dressed woman waiting in the queue at the ticket office.
- Change for a ticket, Miss. Some kids stole my money. I can't get home.
She looks unconvinced.
- Please lend me the money; my parents will post it back to you.
- What's their number? I'll phone them. She takes out her mobile phone. It's small and neat, worth some money. He considers snatching it. She closes her hand over it, as if reading his mind.

Other people in the queue are showing an interest in him now. He's tall for his age, but this crowd is making him feel small and vulnerable. He ducks between two men and runs for it. He hears shouting. They could be after him. He wishes he had a knife to protect himself. That woman would have given him the money if he'd had a knife.

In the street again, he realises it's getting dark. Adrenalin pumping, he scans the road for somewhere to hide. He squats down between some parked cars. It gives him time to think. He listens for the sound of running feet. Nothing. No-one shouting, no-one chasing him. He stands up slowly. He looks around. He stops panting, breathes normally.

Think, think. What have you done? You walked out on Julie. She asked for it. Teach her a lesson. She'll treat you better now. It's not a crime, to walk out like that. But if I stay out any longer she'll have the police after me.

He brushes down his clothes and walks to the next road. Reads the name of the street. He knows where he is, twenty minutes, half an hour at the outside and he'll be back at Julie's. After a block or two he begins to walk faster, thinking of supper … and a block after that he begins to run.

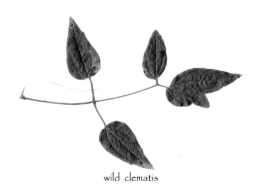

wild clematis

Toni has been a member of Dean Writers' Circle for more than twenty-five years. She has found in it a place where she feels at home with a disparate group of people who share a burning ambition to write and have their work read by others. She started a junior circle, 'Writersaurus', which ran for two years. She presently holds the post of Secretary.

Natalie Williams

THE WRITER

Wendell had just finished picking the big toe on his right foot. "I'm fed up!" he exclaimed. He stood up and began walking, five steps forwards and five steps back, stopping every time he made those five steps only to scratch his ear or poke inside one of his nostrils.

He carried out these actions with his right hand even though under normal circumstances, he boasted about being a left-hander. Not that he would be proclaiming it from the rooftops. The only thing he always insisted on was unlocking the door with his left hand; when meeting people, he ostentatiously tried shaking hands with his right hand on the second attempt; in restaurants he would swap over the knife and fork. He even bought himself a special tin opener for left-handers. His backhand was destructive for all right-handed tennis-players (other than that, he was a rubbish player) and, of course, he signed his name with his left hand. Nobody could begin to suspect how difficult it was to make his signature look elegant and effortless.

The only reason why he had undergone left-hand convert training was that according to statistics, left-handers are brighter, more talented and successful than the right-handed population. Wendell was a statistician. Besides, he knew he was a great writer, at least one of Hemingway's stature. The image of a left-hander suited a future Nobel-prize winner.

"*Bleepbleep! Bleep!*" whispered Wendell passionately and thus enriched the vocabulary of his future novel. He started pacing about again.

Every great writer finds a great love of his life that inspires him, cools his forehead during creative fevers and keeps his body warm when he is shivering with cold. Wendell had decided that before his statistically expected success, he must find and meet such a love.

It all happened the day before yesterday. A very gentle young lady started working for his company. Her name was Danielle and she had just passed her finals at secondary school. As soon as he set his eyes on her, his heart leapt. There was no doubt she was the one.

He invited her for dinner at once. He learnt, above their glasses of Chardonnay, that she was indeed a delicate and sensitive woman.

Yesterday, they went to the opera. She was so excited about the whole Rigoletto story, which made him believe he'd made the right choice. He asked her to go for a walk and then for a cup of tea in his apartment. The tea was never served. Wendell fell on his knees before Danielle and confessed his love for her. He told her that she was the love of his life. He supported his claims with statistical data and calculation of probability of how successful such an investment should become.

Danielle gaped at him and to begin with, she wanted to laugh. However, she soon realised, that it was not meant as a joke when, to her astonishment, she heard that, given Wendell's previous relationships, she – Danielle – with 98.9999998741% was Mrs Right. If she decided to sacrifice herself and become the spouse of an as yet undiscovered genius, his chances of actually receiving a Nobel prize would increase from the original figure of 50.00% to 78.4328647991115 (recurring)%.

What he was going to write was not so important – he was sure the success would come. Danielle could not control herself any longer. She rolled her eyes and burst out laughing. Now it was Wendell's turn to feel confused. What had just happened? Was she ill? Had he said anything amusing?

The young lady calmed down and said coldly, 'You are an idiot, sir.' She turned around and slammed the door behind her. Wendell just stood there, stunned.

Two hours later, his secretary called, complaining that "the new girl has just resigned." Wendell felt a chill spreading all over his body. This was why he had been picking his toe, poking his nose and pacing around the room, while forgetting about being a left-hander.

He was sorry that Danielle had left. She would never come back. His disappointment was slowly going away. His binary brain began working again. He lifted his eyes and looked at the wall-clock. 'The only possibility is that I must have made a mistake in my calculation. Danielle was not the right woman. Well, never mind. I will find someone else soon. And then, at last, I shall become a writer,' mumbled the sixty-four year old boy, then he lay down on his bed and fell fast asleep forever.

bracken

Natalie, born in Czechoslovakia, is currently living with her husband and two dogs in the lovely Forest of Dean, keeps writing in several languages and tries to overcome different obstacles such as driving on the wrong side, fifty-nine sorts of bread in the supermarket (which one is edible?), and how to set mousetraps in the pantry. She remains a hundred per cent Prague lady.

Part Two

Retrospective

Because this is an Anniversary Edition, we are publishing work by retrospective members who, for one reason or another, are no longer with us. It is manifestly obvious that it has not been possible to get in touch with all our previous members. There are those of course whose work we would have loved to include but contact has been lost with so many.

We are most grateful to all those who have contributed to this anthology and to the families of those who have passed on for allowing us to publish their work posthumously.

Chinese Chess

I could not tell you exactly when the deterioration in my social intercourse began, but inevitably, one cannot ignore the trickle of mail drying to a mere plop, unexpected visitors becoming as common as heat waves and the high point on my calendar a visit to the dentist – the whole situation being further aggravated by a lack of convenient and reliable transport coupled with, as modern jargon has it, a cash-flow problem.

Well, I have always considered myself resourceful and I dealt with the dismal daily doormat by sending away for details of loft conversions, retirement policies, made-to-measure curtains – the list of which I may not bore you. Anyway, not only was there a mystery to unfold each morning but also excellent fire-lighting material. As for recreation, I had been in the habit of popping along to the council tip but nowadays, it seemed, there were more persons removing from the area than bringing in, although I still went along to the bottle bank – I suppose it satisfied the laid-back vandal in me. But by far my most favourite haunt, especially in winter, was the local library. So regular were my visits that I had been awarded the status 'favoured borrower' and I was even allowed to replenish the shelves on quiet occasions.

It was, as I can best recall, one particularly dark, wet afternoon in March when, stretching to replace 'The Biography of Abel Skidmore, Founder Member of the Safe Driver Club' that my glance fell upon a four zero dot, dot, amongst the six zero dot, dots. Incensed by this wanton act of anarchy I snatched it down and, inserting it in its rightful place, I could not help but notice the title 'How to Talk to your Cat'.

I should like you to understand that, normally, I would dismiss such things along with photos of dogs sat behind pints of ale wearing cloth caps but, prompted by curiosity, I flipped to the introduction. Ten pages later I was hooked and took it on extended loan. We began lessons the very same day.

Now let me clarify one thing – substitute 'Communicate' for 'Talk' for my own feline never mastered his vocal range, but you will appreciate communication takes many forms – a raised eyebrow, a twitched whisker, so many ways of conveying meaning. You may think the number of topics of mutual interest between cat and man is limited – not so – with my lately acquired 'Dolittle' accomplishment I was to discover a new perspective about my commonplace world. After all, cats move unnoticed and unheeded at any hour - and the revelations about my neighbours would astound you.

When, some months later I returned that little gem to its rightful position on the shelf I found, unbelievably, another book by the same Dr Rosetta, 'Teach your Cat Chinese Chess'. Tell me, is there a better way of spending a winter's evening than enjoying a friendly game of Chinese Chess and catching up with the low-down on one's neighbours?

My furry companion showed a natural aptitude for the game - probably there was some Oriental in him, a Persian predecessor perhaps. I must confess to a certain degree of boredom, initially winning every game, so to counter this I resorted to convoluted tactics and unnecessary risks – then, quite suddenly, I began losing more and more. I tightened up my game with little result – also there was developing a certain rancour between us. One evening when a hotly contested game was snatched in the last few moves I found myself the target of a few well-chosen mews alluding to the so-called superiority of the human race. You can imagine my chagrin being spoken down to by fifteen pounds of mouse-burner. Well, one thing led to another and I heard myself shouting untypical jibes, such as 'why don't you get your hair cut?' and 'two years in the army would do you good' – it ended, I'm ashamed to say, with my upturning the table.

We don't communicate any more – in fact, he has moved in

131

with one of my neighbours which caused me many sleepless nights. Supposing they should discover that book – what might they learn about me?

So if you're thinking of scanning the shelves, don't bother – it is no longer in circulation – scrapped possibly, along with the Index Cards.

Tony Allen

ivy

Tony is a former chairman of the Dean Writers' Circle. He writes with humour and originality, expounding his own peculiar take on the world.

SUMMER TERM

Still softly came the summer stealing on.
The golden backs and glowing faces
Emerged once more among us.
The fine clipped shadows of mornings
Bright with chatter of birds.
The jungle afternoons, and the sultry mass of foliage.
The still hot field, the withered grass.
The scorching sun-baked asphalt.
And the crowded field –
The daisy spattered morning field,
Like some grassy beach
With purring transistors, summer's soft security,
And throbbing sun in a clean scraped sky.
All until the evening when the sunlight spilled
Like honey through the swollen trees,
And drowsy warmth filled up the bowl of silence,
Where hidden intensity had swarmed before.
The muzzy shadows lengthened at the fall of day
Until light faded.
Amid it all, lulled into distant dreams,
We scarcely noticed the year grow old,
That at the peak of summer faces vanished
Never to be seen again among us.
How people faded – like the sun that warmed our bodies,
But didn't return next morning.
And how slowly we all grew up.
And soon it would be our turn.
And when, while we were still laughing,
They slipped away from our hands –

Friends, faces, pupils, teachers.
We still didn't understand –
Until we saw the haze of heat was sliding from our grip,
And colder days were dawning, whiter light was falling
From a greyer morning sky.
We looked for them then
And knew that they were gone.

Cathy Brabazon-Drenning

redwood

Cathy was an original member of the Circle. Her poems illustrate the innocence of childhood in the Forest of Dean. She now lives in Spain.

Ghosts of Our Past

The death of a city is a tragic and terrible thing. It is also exciting and beautiful. I want to tell you what it felt like to be a 'ghost' within an ancient ghost city inside a modern ghost town one week before the latter was blasted to rubble.

In 1985 I met the Chinese woman who was to become my wife, and learnt that white foreigners were casually called 'ghosts', because our pale skin was the colour of death. But when, in October 2002, I arrived in Chung Sing, ghost city of the Three Gorges, I did not feel at home.

When our tour boat pulled up at the jetty a large sign said 'Welcome to Ghost City' in Chinese and English. The massive modern white-painted emperor figure, high on the hillside was clearly visible, but I did not know at that point that this modern ghost town sheltered a more ancient and more important city of the dead. I wondered if the sign had been put up as a bad joke by the residents of Chung Sing, who were having to leave their homes, their memories, their ancestors. I wondered if it was purely British humour, to joke about such a fundamental loss.

The modern city was obviously dying. Buildings were dark and deserted. Good houses were being knocked down. But the city bustled with energy. Shopkeepers and traders stayed until the last moment, until the last tourist had come, spent her money, and gone. Other inhabitants had become scavengers on the body of the dying city, collecting bricks and wood for resale. I saw one family with a tiny tractor and small trailer saving their possessions. They piled it high with a chest of drawers, a table and two chairs, and a mattress, tied them on tight, and drove out of town for the last time. Children ran and played, as if all were normal, but most helped their families. Sell, sell, sell. A massive closing down sale. Everything must go.

We climbed the ancient steps, entered giant carved gateways, and rode the modern chair lift to see the temples of prayer and offering, and the caves where the ancestors of the rich and powerful were once laid to rest. Then I understood and smiled. I was myself a ghost, and I had entered the Ghost city of the ancients at a time when the modern city that had grown up around it had become a ghost city itself. These ancient places are sites of great history and importance. The decision to destroy them must have been very difficult. The debate has gone around the World. My friends and I had argued over it in bars and sitting rooms in Britain,. History versus progress; spirituality against electricity; majestic scenery resisting flood control; the past making way for the future.

I was sad for the spirits of my daughter's ancestors. The Three Gorges were impressive, but I resolved to return when the new lakes were full – vast and beautiful – and the map of China was changed forever.

When we descended from the spiritual places it was dark. No street lights, no road repairs, and our guide gone on ahead. Each side of a single road the shops and traders gave the city the illusion of life, but it was only a few metres deep. Truck after truck pushed by, flashing, beeping, rumbling, like roaring dragons with glowing eyes and choking breath fleeing something yet more terrible.

We had paid our respects to the Old Ones in our hearts. We boarded our boat as the city's modern replacement flashed in neon and laser from across the river. We bid goodbye to Chung Sing and left it to its fate. It was time to look to our own futures.

Roger Brewis

Roger lives in the Forest and writes articles for Science magazines. He has been Chairman of the Circle.

Barbicide

Snip

Did you see it last night? I was amazed I never thought they'd kill her off so soon after all that business with her sister's husband and the daughter running off with the boy from the Queen Vic I suppose she the actress I mean wanted to leave but you wonder why don't you it must be such a good job but then if you've been in it for as long as she has maybe you need a change ...

Snip

When the phone rings in a particular way – long short, long short - I know it's M with another mission for me and its off with the salon tee shirt and inane grin and on with the shades and the silenced pistol. My cover is flawless isn't it? If you only knew how many heads of state I have left in pools of blood while the reins of power are passed to one of the Organisation's yes men. It would make your hair stand ...

Snip

Oh yes I see what you mean it is a bit dry isn't it we'll have to do something about that have you tried the shampoo I mentioned last time one of my other clients has had amazing results with it when she came in I just didn't recognise her but mind you so many things can affect your hair you know if you work in a smoky office or you're feeling a bit stressed ...

Snip

When you leave I'll be able to follow this hairstyle through the crowds as I look down from the roof with a high-powered rifle.

The telescopic sights are so good I can see every hair on the nape of your neck even at three hundred metres. I often smile at the irony of having my finger curled round a hair trigger – it's the kind of thing that only a tabloid journalist ...

Snip

Oh, I know I saw the same article you'd never think it to look at him would you his poor wife mind you I had a client in here only last week she tells me things about her marriage you wouldn't believe and the worst thing is she knows all about it one time she told me this was about a year ago when I was working in the other salon the other woman actually had an appointment at the same time and they were sitting there side by side well the atmosphere was awful and I said to the other girls for God's sake hide the scissors ...

Snip

These scissors cost £364. So sharp that a feather falling on the blades would be sliced neatly in two. They were hand forged in Japan by craftsmen trained in the ancient art of making samurai swords. The steel was quenched in a vat of human blood to give it that armour piercing hardness. If I place the point just here behind your ear and push gently it will break through a thin layer of bone and go straight in to the brain. They say that the Thugs in India used just the same method when they needed to kill someone without leaving a trace. It's quite painless, you won't feel a ...

Snip

Sorry did that sting a bit yes doesn't she look awful it's completely the wrong style I mean her face is far too round but there are so many who just won't listen you try to explain why they'd be better off with something that has a bit more body but they've seen it in Cosmo and no of course not you it's a relief to find someone who trusts us it's as if we just walked in off the street and started cutting everyone forgets about the training we do and all the little tricks of the trade ...

Snip

There is a shrine to Sweeney Todd in the back room you know. Setting-gel candles in black-lacquered skulls burn all day and the air is thick with hairspray incense. When the last customer has dragged her chemically saturated scalp from the salon we go back there and pay homage to the master, whipping ourselves into an orgiastic frenzy with hair extensions and jabbing hair pins into our legs 'till the blood flows. At the height of the ceremony the work experience teenager throws down her dustpan full of hair, rips off her nylon overall and ...

Snip

Sorry what's that? The blue stuff in the jar – Barbicide? Oh it's just a chemical for cleaning the combs and things. I see what you mean, I suppose it does sound a bit sinister but who would want to kill a barber or a hairdresser? We love everybody. We never did anyone any harm. That's right, who would you have to talk to then?

David Caldwell-Evans

David was a member of the Circle for a short time, until his work for television took him back to London.

Searching for the Enemy

Shaking bars driving of cars.
He does crosswords and he reads
biographies, war stories,
watches TV in between:
may upset that cup of tea.
Medication brings relief
to some of his frustrations.
Of younger days sometimes dreams,
and drives horses in his sleep,
shouts out – 'Wo-ah!' Makes her heart leap,
giving her palpitations.
Involuntary kicks:
sleep in separate bedrooms now.
How fortunes change! Fate flicks us
from one life to another,
while snaps bring back memories,
life in the nineteen forties
when he was in the army:
spent some time in Italy.
She, in a Surrey shelter
with small sons heard Ack-Ack guns,
living life helter-skelter.
Then – happy years – Gloucestershire,
the family together,
holidays, walking for miles,
and living in the country.
Now, he cannot walk far, but
does a little gardening,
unable to drive his car.
Takes Madopar for shaking,
still making the most of life.
Enemy – Parkinsonism.

But for the Grace of God

You could not hear
But it was clear
That nothing would deter
Your love of life,
But all the strife
Seemed too much to endure.

Although in pain
Did not complain,
You did not like a fuss.
Your great spirit
And ready wit
Is missed by all of us.

You gave your all
If one should call
On you for helping hand,
But now you're gone
To be alone
It's you would understand.

The years have gone
You've struggled on
Through all adversity,
And suffered much
Did not lose touch
It was your destiny.

To that far place
No-one can trace
You're gone, and now it seems
That you I'll see
Will ever be
Forever in my dreams.

No-one Goes There Anymore

Tree trunk twisted, and bent with age,
Roots anchored into mossy bank,
Like some immortalized old sage
Guarding the spring from which he drank.

From knobbled trunk a silhouette,
A deeply furrowed warrior's face,
Man's image in a tree was set,
Suspension of a time, and place.

A place where many came and went,
The alder tree's outlived them all
In isolated quiet content,
For no-one goes there anymore.

Violet Croad

alder

Violet was an extraordinary poet, prolific in her output and published in numerous national anthologies. The three verses published above can only offer the tiniest taste of her unique style and abilities. She was a long-time loyal member of the Circle who was still attending regularly up to the time of her death.

Per Ardua Ad Astra

I had introduced team-work to 4C very early in my acquaintance with them. The class was divided into Red, Green, Blue and Yellow teams, and good work, behaviour, punctuality and attendance were all rewarded by the presentation of stars in the team colours. In exceptional cases, gold stars were awarded and these were worth ten of the coloured variety. The whole class had to be in agreement with the presentation of this high honour and very few were ever gained.

Joseph was unanimously awarded a gold star for his care of Billy. Joseph was one of the kindest and most helpful boys in 4C; he was the youngest of a large family, and suffered the great disability of a cleft palate, but cheerfully ignored the fact as he helped Dorothy tidy the room, arrange the nature table, or give out books before school.

If Joseph, however, had a disability, there seems no word left to describe Billy's misery. He was a thin, undernourished scrap, who suffered permanently from epileptic fits. These grew more frequent as the year wore on and the poor boy's frailty increased. I insisted that he was seen by the school doctor, who in turn sent him to the hospital. The specialists could do nothing – it was an inoperable tumour of the brain.

Billy's fits were accepted by 4C as part of everyday life. If he were in the classroom it was easy – the nearest child would snatch up a cushion kept for the purpose and put it under his head, while another saw that he could not injure himself by contorting his body and banging himself on the iron legs of the desks and also put a pencil between his teeth to prevent his biting his tongue. When the attacks came on in the playground it was less easy. The first time I saw Billy in the throes of an attack, he was lying in the filthy, muddy playground – almost choking, while the other boys, chasing each other, just jumped over him if he happened to be in the way. I felt sick at what appeared to be their callous indifference. As I bent over him, Joseph rushed up with his coat.

'Is 'e orl right, Miss? I cou'nt git 'ere afore. I'll just put this under 'is 'ed. I always keeps me heyes on 'im at playtime.'

My faith in humanity restored. Joseph not only 'kep' 'is heyes on 'im' at playtime, but walked home with Billy and back to school with him every day. One day one of the bigger boys was making game of both of them, when Joseph said,

'Go hon! Larf at me if yer like – but leave 'im art of it!'

Eventually, Billy was taken to hospital and Joseph collected from everyone for some sweets, which he intended to deliver himself. The authorities would not admit him on account of his age. Back came Joseph and the sweets –

'I di'nt trust 'em wiv 'em Miss. Will yer tike 'em for me?'

'Of course I will, but will you show me where the hospital is?'

'Yis, Miss – but can yer go ternight, cos they said 'e was very sick.'

I must confess that the idea of visiting Billy haunted me all day. I knew how ill he must have been, otherwise the hospital would never have admitted him.

Joseph and I reached the forbidding, Victorian structure – a former workhouse – which served as a general hospital for the area. I left my guide at the enquiry office and set off to Ward 12.

144

The corridors were draughty and bleak, and reeked of disinfectant; the stairs seeming unending. At last I reached my destination and enquired of the Sister as to Billy's whereabouts.

'I don't think he's conscious,' she said, 'you know he's very ill?'

I assured her I did, and that on behalf of my class I had brought a very sticky and entirely unsuitable collection of sweets. Their condition had not been improved by Joseph's refusal to entrust them to the hospital's care on his first visit.

'When he recovers consciousness, tell him Joseph brought them from 4C with their love and best wishes for a speedy recovery.'

Sister nodded.

'Did yer git there in time, miss?' was Joseph's greeting.

'Yes Joseph. He was asleep, but Sister promised faithfully to give them to him when he woke up.'

I thought at the time that Joseph's remarks referred to the end of visiting hours, but later discovered that he knew as well as I did that Billy was not going to recover.

After Billy's death two days later, the leaders of all four teams requested that Joseph and Billy should both be given gold stars.

Heath Cutler

Heath was an English teacher at a local secondary school. She ran a WEA course on Creative Writing, at the end of which some of the participants continued meeting together – so the Dean Writers' Circle was formed. Heath was herself an early member but then moved out of the district. She has since died but fortunately left behind a book describing her early teaching experiences in a North London school. The extract printed above is from that book.

Miss Ethel Lewis

We had been sent to St Stephen's Church in Belle Vue Road, the Vicar being the Rev. Biddle. St Stephen's had a very substantial Church Hall, situated in the Meend District, and served for a good many social occasions.

It was to this hall that we went to Sunday School. St Stephen's was very well supported and the classes were divided according to age and sex. Each group had a devoted teacher who attended regularly every Sunday.

My teacher was Miss Lewis.

Miss Lewis was not designed by nature or occupation to make a charming first impression.

A spinster of uncertain age, very painfully thin, a black dress hung about her, a black hat with whispy hair escaping beneath the brim, weak, slightly bulging pale, blue eyes, with wired framed spectacles, a very clean, scrubbed, bony face with prominent red nose requiring frequent attention from a pocket handkerchief, her wrists also red and bony protruded beneath her cuffs and knuckles also red and over-exposed looking.

Her most unfortunate feature – her teeth, protruding and widely spaced out at the outer edge.

I was told by one of the girls, that Miss Lewis was the maid at the vicarage and did all the cleaning and scrubbing and also looked after the children.

The vicarage was a large rambling house behind the church, with quite extensive lawns and a laurel hedge bordered by St Annal's lane.

I suspect that Miss Lewis's labours at the vicarage did little to fill out the figure or help her catarrh. Cleaning grates and lighting fires on cold winter mornings, scrubbing stone floors and coping with young children, cleaning herself up and dressing in white cap and apron over black dress to be presentable at the front door in the afternoon, was the routine of Miss Lewis's day, day in – day out.

But it was easy to see how much she enjoyed her Sunday School lessons with her young class. I soon forgot her unprepossessing appearance, and enjoyed the opportunity she gave me to read aloud from the Bible Stories we studied in class. One day I came across the expression 'a hand-maiden of the lord', and ever after, in my eyes, Miss Lewis was this person.

When summer holidays came, she would spend her half-day taking us on expeditions, paying for our expenses. We would visit different beauty spots. She once took us on a long walk through the town to the Soudley Rocks, down into the valley, over the brook and a steep climb up the other side.

We had tea on the lawns of an isolated cottage. It was called 'Moss Cottage'. It was a wonderful outing, eating cakes and drinking lemonade, the silent woods all around us, surrounded by giant pines.

We came back on the rail motor. I never could find 'Moss Cottage' again.

Gladys Duberley

lime

This is an extract from Gladys's second volume of life in the Forest of Dean. The first volume was called 'Heaven Lies About Us' and was published by The Forest Bookshop. Unfortunately Gladys died before the second volume was completed. Gladys was an early member of the Circle.

FUNNY OLD SORT OF A DAY

The water went over his head and he knew that he just might die.

It had been a funny old sort of a day all round. As usual, he was late for school. That had been Mum's fault really because she'd felt that she had to iron him a clean shirt, when yesterday's would have done. Then when he'd arrived, Old Hatcher, his year six tutor, went on and on about his time keeping and told him that when he went to the secondary in September they wouldn't put up with it – he'd be in trouble all the time and not just half of it like now.

He did badly in the Maths, the English and the Spelling tests and Old Hatcher had had a go at him about that as well.

'At this rate Johnson, we'll have to set up a Year 'Six A' just for you. You're certainly not ready to play with the big boys yet. Maybe if you got here on time now and again, you'd be doing better. I might have a chat with your parents.'

Mind you, he'd said that to Josh before – about talking to his Mum and Dad – but it had never happened. He'd have a hard job speaking to Dad anyway, because he'd left Mum years ago and lived miles away. He and Mum were divorced now and they never saw him nowadays. He did send Mum some money every month, but still had to go out and get a job. Chrisy still missed him a lot and Josh often heard her crying in the night; but then she'd always been "Daddy's Little Girl". Josh missed him too, but it didn't hurt so much any more.

Mum wouldn't be home from work until five. Still, he had his own front door key – which was cool. Normally, he'd have had to pick up Chrisy from her school so that they could walk home together. Mum liked them to be in doors as soon as possible after school was out – no hanging about. Today, was different. Chrisy was away on a Science Museum trip to London and Mum

148

would be collecting her when the coach got back about six-thirty. As it was a non-homework night, Chas Evans, his best mate, had suggested that after school they spend some time up on the common. The lakes were frozen over and people were skating. It should be a bit of fun. Why not? Mum didn't need to know.

Old Hatcher left half-an-hour early that afternoon and Miss Jenson, the head, stood in for him, keeping them at it right up to the time that the bell went. Chas and Josh carried their books in rucksacks, slung over their shoulders. It was a bit cold. The common was a ten minute walk from school but they trotted there all the way to keep warm and so that they could spend more time watching the skaters. Neither had ever done it themselves but they both had roller blades and weren't bad on them.

There were two small lakes which were used for very little rowing boats in the summer. The water wasn't very deep in either of them. Last April, after football, they'd gone there in their strip, taken off their trainers and waded across both of them from one side to the other and the water never even came up to their chests. Now, 'Turn Pike Pond' was a real lake, with birds and fishermen. You weren't allowed to take a boat out on it and people said it was hundreds of feet deep. It hadn't been made like the other two, but had been there for ever and the park built around it. So people said.

It was too cold for birds and fishermen today, so there weren't any around. Chas had been right: the lake was covered with a thick layer of ice and there were lots of people, grown-ups and children, all dressed up warm, gliding across the surface. Josh suggested they have a go sliding on it, but Chas didn't want to because he'd seen a film where, on a day just like this, a monster had come up and grabbed some kids for dinner. Josh laughed at that and told him he was being a right 'prune'. That was what his mother called him sometimes when he believed things which she said had been made up. It made him chuckle because he reckoned she must be a bit of a 'prune' herself, nearly always believing what he told her – especially some of his over the top excuses.

'I'll go by myself then, chicken!' he'd shouted and clucked as he ran back from the water's edge so that he could hurtle at great speed as far as he could across the lake. His long slide was quite something to see. Out of what little sun was showing behind him, he fell head over heels and rolled like a giant, misshapen bowling ball making a crooked run down the alley, people flying like pins left and right, accompanied by screams and shouts of anger.

And then there was nobody in front of him; they were all scattered behind him. He slid over a circle cut in the ice by countless skaters going round and round and he popped into it, no longer a bowling ball but, more like a red, being potted on the snooker table.

The water went over his head and he knew he just might die. He sank deeper and deeper into the darkness. Then he stopped and started to bob upwards. He aimed himself towards the light. A strong pair of hands grabbed his shoulders and pulled him out. He was shivering with cold and fright.

Then a voice boomed out.

'Well young Johnson, it really hasn't been your day has it? We'd better get you cleaned up and dried out before I take you home. Come on.'

It was Old Hatcher! Josh could have died, and then realised he nearly had. Once he had seen that he was all right, Chas had cleared off while the going was good. He took Josh's rucksack with him.

Wrapped in Mr Hatcher's overcoat, Josh was taken back to school in the teacher's car. There he was stuck under a hot shower, given a warm drink and a change of clothing from the emergency store. Then, he was driven home to face his mother who, on hearing what had happened, grounded him for a month. His mum could be quite tough at times.

It had been a funny old sort of a day all round. It seemed that

Mr Hatcher wasn't as old as all that, not much more than Josh's mum really. They had a long talk about him and his school work, about his being late most mornings, and all the trouble he seemed to be getting in nowadays. Afterwards, Josh must have been in their thoughts a lot because even though he had really improved, and moved on to the secondary school, Mr Hatcher still came round to see his mum to have a chat with her a couple of times a week – sometimes a lot more often.

Paul Forni

This story was written for children.

horse chestnut

Paul was a later arrival to the Circle but very regular despite a gradual deterioration in his health. He was a very strong short story writer and very involved in Circle business. Members are still feeling a sense of loss at his recent death.

151

Life

Life to me was wonderful
A very lucky girl
Found at all the parties
My life a social whirl.

Silk and velvet dresses
A ring upon my hand
To show that I was married
To the ruler of the land.

He courted me in secret
Never were we seen
But my happiness was absolute
The day he made me queen.

As an expectant father
His heart was filled with joy
Which changed to disappointment
When told "It's not a boy."

I pleaded for his mercy
But he turned his head away
Looking quite disgusted
He broke my heart that day.

So now I'm out of favour
His heart I'll never win
My head is all he's after
The head of Anne Boleyn.

common reed

Nola Gardiner

Nola stayed a member for a number of years before family commitments took over. She wrote poetry full of tongue-in-cheek humour, each often having a surprise ending.

SIMPLY NUTS

First

Much of day packing and getting gear ready. Jamie Whatsit, engaging little gargoyle, got his Christmas kite stuck high in the tall chestnut. I went up and got it.

'Cor!' said a passing pensioner, glancing upward, 'Yor muvva musta bina squirrel.'

Second

Grimmish journey. Andy and Audrey met my train. Another two hours by Landrover. Increasing snow as we climbed. Hut warm and welcoming, smelling of peat fires, paraffin, candle wax and the enormous stew assembled by Mike and Joanna. Bron looking radiant, and edible herself. All six of us as hungry as wolves. Mike yarning about baboons high above him rolling rocks down the gully he was climbing in the Drakensburgs. Maybe boss male mistook him for a rival. Audrey says he's cuddly.

Third

Planned easy first day. Up the spur, along the main crest, down by frozen lake, through pine forest and home. Four hours, we thought. It took six.

Roped in twos and threes for safety, but no real climbing. Bitter cold and strong wind. My face burning, then numb. Someone, maybe yesterday, had compressed and compacted the snow beneath each footstep. The wind had since swept all the

153

loose snow from the crest leaving only boot-shaped ice blocks to mark his passage across the bare glazed rock. Andy says only yetis can leave tracks in raised relief like that.

They tell me that my skin has gone black where it was exposed between goggles and face mask.

Fourth

Blackened skin now peeling off. Surface frostbite. Must take more care. Mike and I decided to take the Flake Crack route up Cathedral Peak. It's listed Mild Severe, which seems a contradiction in terms. The Flake is estimated to weigh about 50 tons and is delicately and precariously balanced on a ledge, like a flint spearhead standing on its base. The route means bridging the widening gap for about 40 feet, then up on the outside, very exposed. Then the dreaded step across from the tip to the main wall again. As you step the whole Flake rocks back and forth, making a deep 'clunk, clunk', like a laden trawler nudging a jetty. The movement unnerved Mike who did not like it one little bit. Not so bad for me, used to trees.

Fifth

The tops all hidden in cloud, and thin snow falling like frozen drizzle. The others all had chores to do or books to read.

Decided to walk up the ridge a bit.

'By yourself?' they queried. 'Take care.'

'Sure', I said. 'No risks'.

Forty minutes later the visibility dropped insidiously and almost stealthily. Suddenly I could see only as far as my feet and about six prints leading to them. They might have been floating in the sky and it was like being at the centre of a glass ball filled with milk. A white-out. Could unknowingly have stepped off the edge of the precipice without ever having seen it. Took a step which I thought was upward, and stumbled badly downhill. Turned and retraced my own tracks before they were blown away. So regained safety.

Discussed early Everest history that night, Mallory and Irvine, and M's obsession to get to the summit. 'Because it is there,' he said.

Later both vanished near the top and were never found. *

Sixth

Again opted for an easy day. Tried Red Slabs, listed in the Climbing Guide as poor, unstable and crumbling. None of us knew them. Andy and the girls went up the easy way, round the side, and belayed top ropes to firm rock in case of need. Mike went up the slabs first, surefooted as a spider on a brick wall. I traversed further right, not wanting either him or the stones he dislodged to fall on me. Found a disconcerting depth of fresh air beneath my heels, and a loosened stone fell in silence for long seconds before hitting the waiting rocks below with a sickening crash. Somewhat unnerving. Found a hold for my right hand, tested it gingerly, and a square yard of mosaic-like wall shifted perceptibly outwards. Pushed it gently back into place and called urgently for a top rope. Great relief as one came snaking down and I got a foot into the loop. Then a wheelbarrowful of loose rock from about waist height slipped and plunged down, bruising both legs. Quite a buzz to reflect that without the top rope I'd have plunged down with it.

Coz Roz says that we climb, not because it is there, but because we are simply nuts.

Philip Gurdon

155

This was read by Philip at the Cheltenham Festival of Literature 1993, under the Events Title of **Inside the Diary**.

*At this time the body of Mallory had not yet been discovered.

sweet chestnut

Philip is a former chairman of the Circle. He has published two books recalling his adventures as an airline pilot. Some years ago he moved to Herefordshire.

The Gift

Jessie Fielding would have indignantly denied that she was inquisitive. She preferred to call it taking an interest, yet the fact remained, that very little went on in her neighbourhood that she didn't know about, at least that was until Mrs Wallace moved into the empty house opposite – there she drew a complete blank.

It was weeks before she even managed to find out her name, and then only by asking the milkman outright. It appeared Mrs Wallace had no contact whatever with her neighbours. She did not frequent the bingo hall, the library or the flower club and an invitation to join the W.I. was politely but firmly refused. It seemed her only excursions were the daily walks with her dog Dandy, taken in the morning and evening.

Jessie failed dismally to engage her in conversation. She contrived to be dusting her window ledges as Mrs Wallace passed by.

'There's no keeping this dratted dust down, is there,' she said, with an ingratiating smile. A pair of steel-grey eyes looked into hers, the merest pause, a brief nod, and Mrs Wallace swept on her way. If Jessie was an expert at extracting information, Mrs Wallace was an expert at withholding it.

This went on for some months, the comings and goings of Mrs Wallace becoming an obsession with Jessie. She lost all interest in her other neighbours affairs; her time was spent behind the net curtains in her front room, watching the door opposite.

The lady however remained a complete mystery. As far as Jessie could tell, she had no friends in the area. There were cars that arrived, sometimes in the morning, sometimes at night. Had Mrs Wallace been a younger woman, Jessie could have labelled her a lady of easy virtue, or something equally derogatory, but she looked all of fifty, her hair was silver, her clothes expensively unobtrusive and for all her detached manner, her eyes flashed a warning – keep away.

This state of affairs continued until the day of the accident. Jessie had taken up her post behind the curtains for it was time for Mrs Wallace to take Dandy, her spaniel, for their morning walk. The door opened and Dandy, barking excitedly, ran into the road. Car and dog met with sickening impact, the screech of brakes and pitiful yelping gave Jessie the excuse she had been waiting for. She was out of the house in a flash.

Mrs Wallace was kneeling in the road, supporting the dog in her arms.

'Poor little love,' said Jessie. 'Can I do anything?'

Mrs Wallace looked up. 'Please phone the vet.'

As she ran back into the house, Jessie heard Mrs Wallace say softly to the dog, 'Not long now Dandy.' Silly woman, she thought.

The vet arrived and after a brief examination, took the dog back to his surgery. Jessie privately thought its chances of recovery were slight but did not say so. She turned her attention to Mrs Wallace, white and trembling, her distress was obvious.

'Can I get you a drink, a cup of tea perhaps? You've had quite a shock.'

Mrs Wallace declined but to Jessie's surprise, invited her in for coffee. Never having expected an invitation like this, she accepted with alacrity. While the coffee making was in progress, she looked her fill, taking in every detail of the charmingly furnished lounge. As they sipped their coffee, Jessie attempted to steer the conversation on to a more personal note but found her hostess's steady gaze somewhat disconcerting. Then suddenly, cutting through Jessie's efforts, Mrs Wallace said,

'I'm sure you find my private life interesting Mrs Fielding, but there's no point, I'm leaving quite soon, in fact the arrangements have been made. I'm just waiting for Dandy.'

Ignoring the sarcasm, Jessie pressed on. 'Aren't you happy here? Perhaps if you made a few friends, joined in some of the local activities ...' Her voice trailed away under the other woman's steady gaze. Mrs Wallace smiled.

'I have many friends,' she said and, as if reading Jessie's thoughts, added, 'The people you see arrive by car, come on business.'

There was no way to prolong the conversation; the visit was at an end. Jessie rose to her feet and made for the door but before she could reach it, Mrs Wallace took her arm and looking into her eyes, said, 'I'll see you before I go. I have a gift for you. Goodbye Mrs Fielding!'

Jessie puzzled about the strangeness of Mrs Wallace's words. It was the first time they had talked at length and she couldn't make head nor tail of it. The day passed, dusk settled on the town, it grew dark, nine-o-clock she noticed, drawing the curtains, force of habit causing her to look across the street.

She saw the lights suddenly go out in the house opposite. A small group of people began to leave, a tall man holding a little girl by the hand and an elderly woman. The man turned to look at someone following behind him. It was Mrs Wallace. Around her feet, dancing and jumping up, was Dandy. As she watched, Mrs Wallace paused and looked steadily toward the window where Jessie stood. A moment more and they were gone.

The next day started like any other. Jessie brought in the milk noticing that Mrs Wallace had not collected her's. Later in the morning, after much thought, she decided to give up her pastime of watching Mrs Wallace's every move; there was a movie she wanted to see in the town, she would do some shopping and lunch out first. It was half past six when she stepped off the bus. It was but a short walk to her house. She let herself in, picking up the evening paper on her way.

Two cups of tea later, she remembered the paper still folded near her shopping. As she unfolded it, one headline caught her attention. In thick black type it announced, "Death of Famous Medium". A feeling of unease gripped her: she read on. "Moira

Wallace died at her home last night. The cause of death has not yet been established but it is believed to be due to a faulty electrical appliance. The time of death is estimated at about nine-o-clock yesterday evening."

There followed details of her past achievements, also that Mrs Wallace was widowed, her husband having died years before in a fire at their London home. Their small daughter and her mother had also perished in the same fire.

Ashen faced, Jessie picked up the phone and dialled a number. In answer to her question the vet replied that Mrs Wallace's dog had died last night. In a barely audible whisper, she asked, 'At what time?'

'Nine-o-clock!' was the reply.

Everything fell into place, the words whispered to the injured dog, the lights fusing, the people leaving the house – she had witnessed the exit of Dandy and Mrs Wallace.

With a feeling of dread, she realised the nature of the gift bestowed on her by Mrs Wallace, and she didn't like it, not one little bit.

Ursula Humphries

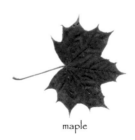

maple

Ursula joined the Circle very early on in our existence and stayed with us for many years. Eventually, she found her strong commitments to the British Legion left her little time for writing. She still lives locally.

Phoney

See that guy on the street,
Gucci shoes on his feet, He's so smug,
He's so neat
You can tell he's replete
With a laptop, a Jag
And a cool menthol fag,
So why does he brag
On his mobile 'phone,
'Bout his life,
Sexy wife,
City strife,
Edge of knife?
Oh, his time's so expensive,
His mind's never pensive
His language offensive,
He chats to his mates,
Says 'Can't stop, I'll be late
For lunch with Bill Gates,
He'll be really irate.'
So he talks
As he walks
Pushing people, he squawks
At a joke, waves a twenty-
Big Issue, 'I've plenty
Of money', Silk ties
It's so funny, he buys
Costly sushi, disguised
By his Ray-Bans he lies
As he tries to sound clever,
Ignores me, he never
Says sorry, he pushes

Past mothers, past babies
Past well pregnant ladies,
He strides, he parades his
Importance, he made his
Big money through stress
So I couldn't care less
'Bout his website address
As I stick my foot out
And shout, 'Oi, you smug prick!'
And he talks as he trips
And he looks such a pratt
And he lands with a splat,
And I think, 'Well, that's that.'
Then, from inside my suit
Comes a beep, so I root
In my jacket, I fumble
And blush as I mumble,
'Hi Mum, how are you?'
And I hurry, push through
Ageing women in queues
'Cos time's money, and I'm so
Important, expensive,
My skills are extensive,
I'm not apprehensive
About meeting Bill Gates
For a business lunch date,
Lose the deal if I'm late.

Paula Jennings

Paula was once secretary of the Circle. She edited and published
Forest Leaves 3, almost single-handedly.   She now lives in
Gloucester.

The Nursery

'Once upon a time,' said mummy Norah, 'there were giants living on the Earth. But they went away and, for thousands of years, the world belonged to us. The sun warmed us and we lived in a garden where fruits grew on the trees. Everyone was very happy then ...'

Davy stirred, raised his head from the pillow of her breasts, and gazed up at her. He was happy now, under the heat-lights in the nursery shed, knowing no different. He had learned to walk and talk and use the latrine, and had all he needed – food enough to sustain him and mummy Norah to love and raise him. He had forgotten the natural mother who had born and suckled him, the pain of separation. Gently, mummy Norah removed the thumb from his mouth.

'Poor little mite,' she murmured.

'It doesn't do to get too fond of them,' mummy Rose reminded her. Mummy Norah sighed. After ten years in the breeding sheds and parting with a dozen babies in succession, it was hard not to grow fond of the youngsters in her care. Murmurous, in the crowded spaces around her, a dozen adult women fostered as she did and grew equally fond. And, for all her advice to the contrary, no one was more loving than mummy Rose. Little ones chose her, clung to her, snuggled against her naked flesh, or slept within the crook of her arm. She grieved for all of them when they left, just as mummy Norah would grieve for Davy.

She searched his hair for lice. Perhaps, she thought, he was too young for stories. But the child on mummy Rose's lap was somewhat older. At four years she was ready to be transferred to the growing shed. Bright blue eyes were fixed on mummy Norah's face, intent and listening.

'What happened next?' she demanded.

'The giants came back,' mummy Norah informed her.

'They're ogres, not giants,' said the child.

'Who told you that?' asked mummy Rose.

'Sometimes, when you think I'm asleep, I hear you talking.'

'That's naughty, Susan!' Mummy Rose's voice was unusually stern. 'You're not supposed to eavesdrop on private conversations! You'll end up with ears the size of sauruses.'

'What's sauruses?' asked Davy.

'Huge enormous animals,' said mummy Norah.

'With huge enormous ears,' mummy Rose added.

'They pull carts and plough the fields,' said mummy Norah. 'And the ogres ride on them when they go hunting.'

Susan pondered for a moment, scratched the flea-bites on her leg. The straw was alive with vermin, unchanged for over a week and stinking of baby dung and urine. Rats fed at night on spilt morsels of food.

'Mummy Cheryl said the ogres eat us,' Susan announced.

'Rubbish,' said mummy Rose.

'Of course they don't eat us,' mummy Norah confirmed.

'She said, when we begin to grow up we'll be sent to the fattening shed. And after that we'll be taken to the slaughter-house.'

Fear flickered in mummy Rose's eyes. There were lines of age on her face and her hair was streaked with grey. For her the ending Susan had spoken of was not far away. But she would not let a young child live with such knowledge.

'Now listen, sweetheart,' mummy Rose said gently. 'I've explained to you before. When you leave here you go to the growing shed. You'll have lots of other children to play with and plenty of room to run about. You've got years to enjoy yourself yet. And mummy Cheryl was talking nonsense.'

'She ought to know better,' mummy Norah agreed.

Mummy Rose picked a flea from Susan's arm and squashed it. A small child screamed at the other end of the shed. Others nearby crawled or toddled through the reeking straw. It was close to feeding time and they were restless. Other mums with their broods gathered by the row of troughs.

'Din-dins,' Davy said eagerly.

'Dinner,' mummy Norah corrected.

'He's stupid,' said Susan.

'No I'm not!'

Scrambling from mummy Norah's lap, Davy thumped her with his fist on her bare thigh. Yelling and furious, Susan thumped him back and kicked him when he fell. His howls were louder than the hooves of sauruses on the cobbles of the yard, the rattle of cart wheels and the ostler's heavy tread. Small children scattered as mummy Rose leapt to her feet, gripped Susan's arm and pulled her away.

'Enough of that, Missy!'

'Pick on someone your own age!' mummy Norah said indignantly.

'He hit me first,' shrieked Susan.

The barn doors opened letting in a blast of cold light. And the ogre keepers followed, towering silhouettes against the outside brightness. Buckets clattered and a slop of milky porridge was tipped into the troughs. Picking Davy up and wiping his tears, mummy Norah elbowed her way through the crush. But Susan fought like a child demented, oblivious to everything, shrieking and struggling in mummy Rose's arms.

One of the ogres spotted them. A great voice clakked, and huge booted feet stepped across the straw. The heat-lights swung as he bent beneath them. His head-crest was raised and the tip of his tail lashed angrily. Strong, slender fingers prised the woman and child apart. One hand set Susan carefully on her feet, the other hoisted mummy Rose high in the air for a closer look. He must have seen what mummy Norah noticed earlier – greying hair and wrinkles, the signs of ageing – an old brood woman who had outlived her usefulness. Tucking her beneath his arm, the ogre

165

carried mummy Rose away.

A terrible silence filled the shed. Mummy Norah could hear the rustle of the ogre's thermal overalls, its boots clomping on the cobbles. She could hear the sauruses breathing outside in the yard, a song bird singing, the soft soughing of the wind and mummy Rose weeping. There was nothing she could do.

But with a cry of rage as the doors began to close, Susan launched herself. She was barely as high as the ogre's knee, her screams to him no louder than a gnat's whine, her words no more intelligible, her pummelling fists a mere irritation. He simply clakked like an irritated rooster in his unpronounceable language, scooped her up beneath his other arm and strode away.

Davy sobbed in mummy Norah's arms. It was the ogres who had scared him, not what had happened. He was too young yet to understand – but from the lives of the foster mums and the nursery shed, Susan and mummy Rose were gone for ever.

Louise Lawrence

wild cherry (autumn)

Louise, a former chairman of the Circle, was responsible for writing, producing and making the costumes for several of our original pantomimes which were well-received by the public. She now lives in Co-Mayo, Ireland.

THE PRIEST'S TALE

Dusk is descending. Several 'down and outs' drift toward their favourite park benches to secure themselves a base for the night. Many vagrants clutch parcels containing bread and, dripping, and if they've been lucky, a potato or two.

Father O'Reilly settles himself on a pew under an oak tree, and prays for a dry night. The sky is difficult to read, as the nearby power station and numerous mills belch out their filth into the atmosphere, creating grey clouds which hang ubiquitously over the dismal landscape below. Salford had enjoyed a rain-free week, which in itself is a miracle, let alone in November.

The elderly skinny priest watches the tramps enjoying the respite from the rain. Tattered coats are used to sit on, rather than worn, and boots are removed for comfort. The feast begins. The food is probably the result of a day's begging from the residents who inhabit the back-to-back terraced houses set in the cobbled streets which surround the park as a maze. They are friendly, kindly folk in this community, and they embrace all faiths – Jewish, Catholic, Protestant. The children of each faith mix freely, without hostility, all playing together in harmony in the dimly lit back entries. It is a community which understands hardship and no-one is ever turned away when they ask a neighbour for help. Gypsies and tramps are an integral part of this society and never go away empty handed. Salford is their hotel.

Father O'Reilly puffs on his pipe, as he reflects on heavenly matters. His thoughts are interrupted by an illustrious character of the area, Smoky by name, who stoops to wish him good evening. Smoky, a kind-hearted if misguided soul, acquired his name because of his unfortunate habit of throwing lighted matches into rubbish bins, just to see what would happen. He had witnessed many a fiery furnace in time. Smoky offers Father O'Reilly a swig from his bottle.

'No thanks, Smoky, old friend,' says the priest sadly, knowing only too well what strong Irish whisky can do to a man, but it takes all the priest's courage to refuse the kind offering. Smoky takes the rebuff with good grace, shrugs his shoulders, and meanders across the park zig-zag fashion, in search of a recipient who may accede to his gesture of hospitality.

Father O'Reilly clasps the crucifix which hangs precariously around his neck and mutters a prayer. He thrusts a hand into the pocket of his ragged robe and extracts a pocket-sized bible, which he opens at random, a ritual the priest has enacted every night for the past five years. He reads a line in the half-light of the twilight zone which he inhabits and the words appear to mock him.

'The meek shall inherit the earth,' he reads. He slams shut his persecutor. 'Irony indeed,' he muses. His reveries are shattered by the sound of a popping cork. He turns, and his eyes are met by the sight of a living, breathing bag of rags in the act of consuming the contents of a grimy bottle. The liquid oozes into the tramp's maw, gurgling on its journey towards the man's septic tank, emitting a putrid stench as he belches, grinning.

Father O'Reilly does not feel revulsion or disgust as he watches the spectacle before him. In fact, he is not sure what emotions the man beside him does evoke. Pity and compassion, certainly, but fear looms its ugly head too. The priest feels certain that he knows the man under the rags, and filth, and hair. Deja-vu. He has experienced this situation before. But no, it is not possible, he thinks. The lateness of the hour and his hunger are whipping up wild imaginings. The priest orders himself to be calm, but still his gut instinct is trying to tell him something, and he knows from past perception that he must be heedful.

'Fine night for sleeping under the stars, my friend.' Father O'Reilly utters gently, as a way of furthering his acquaintance with the tramp. The vagrant looks up, and for one second the priest thinks he sees fear in the eyes of the other. Father O'Reilly offers him a cigarette to show his good intentions. The tramp grunts and relaxes in his seat.

'My name's Sean, Sean O'Reilly,' says the priest, using his Christian name to put him at ease, and offers his hand as he does so. The vagrant accepts the goodwill gesture, and places his grubby hand into that of the priest.

'Cody, they call me,' he says in a husky accent. 'I'll be leaving you in a moment, when I've smoked this cigarette.'

There is a hint of suspicion in the man's voice, so the priest says quickly, 'No, not at all, it's good to have a companion, especially one such as yourself from the old country. We could pass a pleasant hour telling a tale or two now, couldn't we? Tell me, if I may be so bold as to enquire how you came to be in this place, on this night. You tell me your story, Cody, and I'll reciprocate. It's fair exchange now, isn't it? And it will cheer us both up.'

There is a pause. 'Well, it seems fair enough, father.' Cody hesitates. 'I'll call you father, what with your robes an' cross and all, if you don't mind. I don't know where to begin, and that's right enough father, but I'll try to start at the beginning.'

The priest nods, spurring him on.

'Well, 'twas like this – some years ago I, like yourself, was a priest, believe it or not. Ay, a respected member of the community, with decent lodgings, and a fine church to preach in. But I became too high and mighty, and began to forget the purpose of a priest's mission. In short, father, I created my own little kingdom, and used religion to further my own ends. My church was full of respectable people who only paid lip service to the Catholic religion, and attended mass to be seen by their neighbours as being good honest citizens, do you see?

But one evening, an avenging angel appeared in the form of a poor unfortunate vagrant. It was after mass and everyone had returned to their homes to feed their bellies after their spiritual experience. The vagrant entered my church – You see my arrogance father – I still call it *my* church! God forgive me.'

169

Cody makes the sign of the cross.

'As I was saying ... now, where was I ... Forgive my digression. Oh yes. He entered the church, and appealed, no – begged me for help. The poor starving creature asked me for ten shillings for a cup of tea and some food for his belly, as he hadn't eaten in days. I'm ashamed to say father, that I feared the wretch might be seen in such a respectable place of worship and would frighten away the regulars, so to speak. So I told him to be off.

The man glared at me with contempt in his eyes, and lunged at me like a demented animal. He knocked me unconscious with a bottle he had been carrying, and when I regained consciousness, I found the church had been ransacked, and everything of value had been stolen. The scoundrel had gone, of course. Then I came to the realisation that I was naked apart from a tattered overcoat that had been placed over me. My pride was hurt, but no bones were broken. I managed to creep next door to my lodgings unseen – God be praised.

I did nothing but meditate that night. I needed to collect my thoughts. I began to understand how my callousness had contributed towards the way the man had acted. I made the decision to find that man, and apologise. Find him in order to make amends. I felt ashamed that I had not even the compassion to share a meal, and a drink with the man.

So I gave up the church, and took to a life of poverty and privation. I went on a journey to hell seeking him out, and all to no avail. To be honest, when I first saw your robes and your crucifix, I felt fear, and anticipation of who you may be. You reminded me of my old life. Well, there you have it father, the whole unadulterated truth. And now father, what is your story?'

The priest smiles faintly under his black beard, and asks Cody if he may share his bottle. 'No father, it is all I have now.'

There is silence. Father O'Reilly stands up, clasps his crucifix, and begins to speak. 'I have been on a journey to hell too, Cody. I spent all the money I stole from you on drink, and became a tortured soul in my shame. I too swore I would find the man who changed my life five years ago. These robes have brought me nothing but misery – not the respect I always craved.' With that, Father O'Reilly grabs the bottle from Cody and brings it crashing down on Cody's head.

In the morning, Cody awakens naked. A tattered priest's robe has been thrown over him as a blanket. His father confessor has long since gone. Deja-vu.

Maggie Lawrence

gold-leaved holly

Maggie was a member for many years before moving out of the county. She is a librarian, now resident in Hereford but keeping in regular contact with her Circle friends.

The Dance

A dappled light,
flickering,
reflecting,
rising in the spiral shaft.
Shadows dancing,
trembling,
tumbling,
lighting on a mossy path.
Supine forms of
awesome glamour,
cast upon the
hues of green.
Worlds away from temporal clamour,
occupy a world
unseen.
Slipping through a
sun stroked light-shaft,
to glowing
verdant nettle heads.
Sunlight catches on the wings,
which glow and glow
and spread and spread,
then pause to shed
a delicate tracery
overhead.
A picture hazed by sun
bright light.
Catching the moment,
if catch it could,
the intimate dance
of the
Speckled Wood.

Unsung Heroes

I know my black-faced provider,
with his creases and wrinkles and cracks.
I know of his call for the cleansing,
well water washing black backs.
I know the feel of the washing
of the turning of blackness to light.
And I know when the smiles turn to nightmares,
in the sulky deep depths of the night.
My place is to give him some solace,
white collars and wifely aired shirts.
My place is to carry the water
and to not mind my own muddy skirts.
Yes, I know the Black-faced Provider,
who lives in the deep, out of sight.
My own daily life must accept this
and still turn his darkness
to light.

Heather Randall

heather

Heather has been the chairman of the Circle. Her Forest
Diary will be familiar to many listeners of Severn Sound Radio.
An ex-librarian, she was a member for many years. She and Toni
often enlivened our parties with their original sketches, always
performed in fancy dress.

'ON AND OFF THE WAGON'

When an American delegation from Alcoholics Anonymous came to Dublin in the forties, to offer to help us with our drinking problem, the Department of Health inquired, 'What drinking problem?' Other bodies approached sang the same song, 'Mind your own business'.

Fortunately for the many who were to benefit later, an enlightened psychiatrist contacted the delegation. 'Come with me,' he told them, 'and I'll show you the problem.' He took them to St. Pat's, the city's main hospital for alcoholics, warning them that what they would see was just the tip of the iceberg.

Two days later an announcement appeared in the Press which had Irishmen all over the country laughing. Weren't the Americans naïve? But their women weren't laughing; they scented salvation.

The announcement read: ALCOHOLICS ANONYMOUS (US DIVISION) WILL HOLD A MEETING IN DUBLIN'S SHELBOURNE HOTEL ON FEBRUARY 2 AT 8PM. REFRESHMENTS. ALL WELCOME. ADMISSION FREE.

My father laughed, then handing the paper to my mother, said, 'Read that, Nancy. There'll be a queue a mile long for tea and biscuits.'

I was surprised that my mother read the announcement twice. She usually ignored anything that made JP laugh, suspecting his warped sense of humour. 'Good idea,' she said, 'I'll drive you there.'

JP laughed and winked at me. 'Your poor mother's not well.'

My poor mother and I spent the next few days trying to think of a way to make him go to the meeting. To no avail. Then she had an idea that stopped him smiling. 'I need a break,' she said. 'I think I'll go and stay with Bridget.'

As her sister lived in Texas and Nancy had stayed with her before when things got too much for her, it was no idle threat. However, JP, choosing to misinterpret her motive, suggested she took her break in Rosslare, a resort he knew she liked in County Wexford. 'I'll come with you,' he said comfortably, 'we'll have a great time.'

Ignoring his suggestion, Nancy said she would stay a month to make it worth the fare.

'You can't leave me for a month!'

'You'll be fine,' said Nancy, 'I'll get Imelda in to cook for you and keep an eye on things.' Imelda, a neighbour, was anathema to JP.

'She won't get past the door!' he cried. 'I told you, she takes advantage. She's all over me.'

'Only in your mind.' Nancy knew that Imelda had more sex at home than she could handle.

'Well,' said JP, 'she had the opportunity and I wasn't myself!'

'There's logic for you.' said Nancy. 'Wouldn't he make a great lawyer?'

JP then appealed to me to make my mother see sense, but I backed her up. 'You're in this together!' he yelled 'It's nothing but blackmail! I ought to have known you'd be up to something. All right, I'll go to your damn meeting, but only for a joke, so I can tell the lads.' The lads were his local drinking companions. 'But I'll go on my own. I'll have nothing more to do with a low cunning woman like you. I wish I'd never met you!'

'And the same to you!'

I knew they didn't mean it. They'd had a great life together till JP had started drinking. Always laughing and joking and disappearing to make love. If only JP made an effort maybe they could have it again.

For the next few days Nancy went around the house singing in anticipation of her husband's total abstinence and the difference it would make to her life. She could play golf without worrying about the house going on fire, if one of his cigarettes missed the ashtray, and could look forward to a good night's sleep. As it was, she kept vigil for his drunken return, sometimes accompanied by a garda, who was happy to accept a 'jar' for his trouble. As one jar inevitably led to another, one night JP passed out, giving Nancy an opportunity to have a word with his escort.

'Next time,' she told him, 'don't bother to bring him home. Lock him up instead. Maybe that'll cure him.' The look the garda gave her left her in no doubt where his sympathies lay. No wonder the poor man drank.

Nancy now decided that if JP didn't give up drinking she would demand his total absence.

The day before the meeting, fearing JP might back down, Nancy asked a friend of mine, a reformed alcoholic, if he would accompany JP? My friend agreed, provided I came as well. So the following evening the three of us set off for The Shelbourne, JP in a rage at my mother's duplicity.

As we waited in the foyer, JP, looking for trouble, interrupted a couple in front of us who were having an argument; the man wanted to have drink before going to the meeting, the woman objected. Happy to put his oar in, JP said to the woman, 'Dear lady, excuse me, but perhaps I can help. You see, before a lecture on temperance one needs an anaesthetic. May I invite your husband to join me for a drink?' He must have thought asking her permission would do the trick.

Her husband agreed instantly, the lady said no. As the argument continued I was obliged to mention holidays in Texas before JP climbed down. On our way in to the meeting he warned, 'Don't sit anywhere near me.'

About thirty people had turned up, most of them women, including a group of nuns in full regalia. On seeing them JP, no fan of the clergy, said they should be at home praying instead of meddling in things that didn't concern them. The nuns were from an order which took care of alcoholics.

JP sat by the door, my friend beside him. I sat a few seats away next to a very small man who had bruises on his face. He and my friend acknowledged each other. I found out later that the little man's wife knocked him about.

The meeting was late starting, the audience restive, JP threatening to sing 'Why are we waiting?' As the room could have accommodated at least two hundred, I hoped the organisers weren't delaying things deliberately, expecting to fill it. Just then a man wearing a dog collar was ushered in, his purple sash signifying his importance. The nuns rose to greet him; the monsignor had arrived. JP leaned over to tell me he was JC's rep. It took me a while to work out he didn't mean Our Lord in heaven, but our own John Charles, archbishop of Dublin, irreverently known as 'Fingers' (McQuaid) because he had one in everything.

The monsignor settled, the leader of the delegation declared the meeting open, then introduced himself. 'My name is O'Flaherty' he said 'and my folks came from Sligo.'

Applause all round, (sure weren't all Americans Irish?) He went on to give a short history of AA, adding that he hoped the Irish people would join him in their fight against alcoholism. One woman shouted, 'It's the scourge of this country! A national disgrace!' Delighted with her response, O'Flaherty told her they had come here to help us remove the scourge.

The confessions began. A delegate spoke of the misery he had caused his family and friends before joining AA. Identifying with the misery, the women nodded to each other and one elderly gentleman bowed his head. But when a second delegate confessed to losing his wife and child because of his drinking, a man in the audience jumped up and said he always got a great welcome home. No matter what state he was in, his family were delighted to see him.

'That's what you think!' shouted a woman.

When a third delegate listed all the jobs he'd been fired from, a man with a beer belly laughed out loud. 'If you were fired in this country for taking a drop, sure the whole place would shut down!'

Applause from the imbibers.

'Shame!' from the abstainers.

Black looks from the clergy.

At this point there was a break for tea and biscuits, and a rush for the door by men gasping for a jar, including the one we'd met in the foyer and the little man with the bruises.

JP was stopped by my friend, who suggested tea.

'I'm not drinking that muck. I'm off to the lav.'

'I'll come with you.'

Looking around me, I saw a man collecting leaflets. 'Alibis,' he confided, 'I'm with the lads in the bar.' I remembered seeing some macho types heading there on arrival. They would probably spend the night drinking, none of them prepared to lose face.

JP returned, angry. 'Get rid of that fellow. I'm fed up with being followed.' He turned back towards the door and, pretending to chat en route, kept looking at me over his shoulder. I alerted my friend and we followed him.

By now the Rambos in the bar were 'airborne', jeering at the cissies who had come from the meeting.

'Is it lemonade you're after?'

'Sucking up to the yanks!'

'Afraid of your old ladies?'

The little man with the bruises fled the scene, followed by my friend and me and a protesting JP, whom I had blackmailed into submission by mentioning Imelda.

They were still having tea when we got back to the meeting, the delegates surrounded by the nuns and monsignor, whose lively homily on abstinence was soon interrupted when the little man with the bruises, reaching for a leaflet, lost his balance and fell. A delegate rushed to help him, followed by JP, who, seizing his

178

chance to escape, offered to put him in a taxi. But my friend, at his elbow, said to leave it to him, he knew where he lived.

'I'll come with you,' said JP.

'No, we can't both leave. Noblesse oblige.' JP muttered, then glaring at me, said 'Where did you find him?'

Tea and biscuits dispensed, Mr O'Flaherty asked if there were any questions? No questions, so he suggested they elect officers for the Dublin branch. Would the monsignor do them the honour of becoming their president? Of course he would. No surprise there. As by now there were only three Irishmen left in the room, including my friend who had just returned, O'Flaherty asked him if he would become hon. Secretary. My friend agreed; then, sizing up the situation, he proposed JP for treasurer. JP signalled 'No' and kept on refusing until, worn down by the pressure from my friend and the delegates, he eventually gave in and joined them on the platform. O'Flaherty then announced that the psychiatrist who had helped them to get things started had agreed to be chairman. It was significant that the nuns and the other women present were not invited to participate.

And so, their mission accomplished, the delegates went their way and the little man with the bruises went home to another beating.

JP, overcome by all the attention, couldn't wait to give Nancy his version of events. The place was packed, he told her, and though stiff with accountants, he had been chosen to look after the finance. Nancy, delighted, hugged him warmly and urged him to get on with reading the AA booklet. JP, unaccustomed to concentrating – he only read newspapers – had to pin down each page to keep it flat and when he lost the thread, which was most of the time, he blamed our cat, Cosmo, for purring too loudly.

Eventually, the contents of the booklet absorbed, JP waited, sober and irritable, for the subscriptions to come in, as only two had arrived by the end of the week, his interest waned. At which point Nancy, ever-resourceful, contacted the new chairman, (the

179

enlightened psychiatrist) and asked him to invite her husband to speak at the inaugural meeting. So, puffed up with pride and elegant in a new suit, JP regaled his audience with alcoholic reminiscences which, though largely fictional, went down so well they became a regular feature. Until – the lure of the pub overcame his good intentions.

And Nancy was back to entertaining the gardai.

Olivia Rowan

rowan (autumn)

Olivia is known mainly for her plays. The above is part of a series of stories about her father, written for broadcasting. She returned to live in her native Ireland in 2000. She is a life-member of the Circle.

SISTERLY CONCERN

She said they'd be back today, the pair of them. Thursday at 2.30, that's what she said. It is nearly 2.30 now so they are due any minute. Actually I've been expecting HER back ever since she left here on Monday. As a matter of fact I've been sitting in front of this window most of the time waiting for her to walk up that garden path. I was sure she would be back before three days were up. But it seems she stuck it out. Be too embarrassing to leave before the end, I suppose.

Now I'm staying here just long enough to judge what sort of state she's in and then I'll make a dash for it upstairs or out into the kitchen because I certainly don't want her thinking that I care a tuppeny cuss HOW she behaves OR that she's the talk of the neighbourhood. I can see the looks, I can hear the tongues wagging and I'm pretty sure I won't be the ONLY one peering through the curtain, people around here haven't anything better to do or to gossip about.

I know she's my sister and all, but she can be really stupid sometimes. I honestly believe she thinks something is going to come of all this ... at her time of life too ... I suppose when it comes right down to it she's always been dreaming of some Prince Charming or other coming along to carry her off. Still a starry-eyed innocent, poor thing. Should have had MY experience. I've got no illusions about men. I know only too well exactly what a man is after and it is not a middle-aged virgin, that's for sure.

I keep telling her but she won't listen.

I won't deny that he's quite personable. Him a vicar and all. Been here a couple of times on days I knew she'd be out but he made some excuse or other and I'm not the one to go chasing after a man, not like some I could mention.

It makes me squirm when I think about it. A brand new hat and coat she bought, for church ... not before time, I suppose, first

181

one for ten years or more ... and BOOTS! Fancy her buying boots, never worn boots like that before, green wellingtons more her style not those black leather monstrosities right up to her knees.

Disgusting really at her time of life.

And I could not believe it when they said that both of them were going off together for three days, to Bournemouth ... Some religious seminar, supposed to be. Carnal knowledge, that's what goes on at these seminars, everyone knows that and I doubt whether it makes any difference that it is supposed to be religion that they're on about. She'll NEVER cope with it, I dread to think how it's going to end. Be back in floods of tears, I shouldn't wonder and it will be to your's truly to pick up the pieces. HE'LL get the rough side of my tongue, no doubt about that and she won't get a lot of sympathy either. It is not as though I didn't warn her ... Still she's always been a romantic. Read poetry, she's always reading poetry. Oh well I'd better not be too hard on her because we've only got each other after all.

Oooh! Is that the car I can hear? Yes, sounds like it. I've arranged the curtain just right so that I'll be able to see her as soon as she comes through the gate ... I know her so well I'll be able to tell what sort of mood she's in just by the droop of her shoulders. Be sobbing her socks off, most likely ...

They're taking their time, a job to get the cases out of the boot, probably. I expect he'll just drop her off, he won't have the nerve to come in ...

Oh here she comes. I can hardly see her, she's loaded to the teeth with parcels and books and flowers ... She keeps dropping things. Now her hat's blown off and he's chasing after it. Now he's helping her pick up the things ...

Good God they're LAUGHING ... Now he's got his arm round her waist. I don't believe this ... They are behaving like a couple of teenagers.

It's disgusting.

End of Term

When shades of night are falling fast
Who gathers round on new-mown grass?
Who keeps an annual rendezvous
To cook upon the barbecue?
    THE CIRCLE

And who arrives sharp on time,
Laden down with booze and wine,
Clutching tight the latest piece
That each must read before the feast?
    THE CIRCLE

And who, for a year with desperation,
Has struggled with words and imagination,
Written reams, discarded most
And who, tonight, deserves a toast?
    THE CIRCLE

Vera Smith

elder

Vera is our oldest living member, at ninety-two. Despite being very debilitated following a stroke, she is still writing letters. She was made a life-time member when she had to leave the Circle through ill-health.

If I could write the Future

If I could write the future I would slowly spell your name
I'd write it big on the star-sneezed sky
And small on every silver spiderling
And medium-sized on every square of the calendar
Until the day I can't remember how to spell.

I would scribble my name all over your life
Spray-paint your bones, and graffiti your soul
Illustrate your eyes and colour in your heart
And, using my best joined-up writing
I would trace it up your thighs with the tip of my tongue.

Sheila Taylor

elm

Sheila has been a recent member of the Circle. She writes both
poetry and prose. She has also written a novel. This short poem
reflects the depth and intensity of her writing.

The Strange Case of the Missing Gnomes

Mankind, I would say, is divided between those people who like garden gnomes and those who don't. I belong to the latter. I hate them. Some have happy expressions on their faces, and this can't be genuine, standing out in the garden in all weathers, night and day. Others appear to sneer, others to frown.

I think I could stomach a colony of troglodytes, or trogs as they call them, better. They are downright nasty-looking, and don't pretend to be anything else. That is what I told my wife, Sue, when our neighbour had a shipment of gnomes and spread them all around their front gardens.

'The back garden would be bad enough, but in the front I can't help seeing them whenever I go in and out of the house,' I went on.

'Calm down, Alan,' smiled Sue. 'They are not as bad as all that. They could have concreted the whole of the garden and that would have looked far worse.'

I said nothing further but my feelings about these things grew stronger and stronger. I suppose you would call it an obsession. I'm pushing fifty-five and at that age you do get obsessions if you're not careful. I couldn't ask Hugh Bradshaw to remove them as he obviously regarded them with affection. Actually he gave them all names and I've seen him talking to them.

I came to the conclusion that the only way for me to save my sanity was to remove them myself. This, of course, was not easy, but the opportunity did come.

One day in mid-winter Hugh was chatting to me in the street and said, 'The wife's getting a bit run-down. I think a holiday would do her good so I'm taking her away for a long weekend at the seaside. I know it's winter but the air should be clean.'

I refrained from saying it was probably the sight of the

gnomes that was getting her down, and simply remarked, 'Marvellous idea. Enjoy yourselves.'

So there it was, a heaven-sent opportunity and I took it. Everything favoured me. That Saturday night was pitch black and I waited until after midnight before creeping quietly out and letting myself into his front garden with four large plastic bags in my hand.

Of course, Sue was almost beside herself with worry. 'You'll be picked up. I won't visit you in prison,' she kept repeating, but my mind was made up.

Once in the garden with a small torch, well shaded, I was able to pick up those ghastly gnomes rapidly and put them in the four sacks. There were twenty in all so five to a sack worked quite nicely. Then I took them to my garage, one bag at a time, locked two in the boot of my car, and put two on the back seat, discreetly covered.

The whole operation was over in half an hour and I went to bed, well satisfied. Here I was being cunning. Instead of taking the car in the middle of that night to dispose of them, and attracting attention from my neighbours, I left them in my locked garage.

I knew exactly where I was going to lose those objects. This was in a reservoir half a mile away, on the edge of our small town. So the next evening, on the Sunday, fairly late, I drove gently out to the reservoir, pulled up at a particularly dark, deserted spot, and dropped each bag, carefully weighted to make sure, into the water.

I saw each one disappear and felt a glow of satisfaction and no remorse at all at having drowned those beastly objects.

I had my rough collie, Ginny, with me and took her for a brief walk on the reservoir bank to provide myself with a reason for being there, but saw no one. I thought one of our neighbours might have reported the absence of those gnomes sometime that day, but apparently nobody had, for there was no police activity. So it wasn't until Hugh got back on Monday afternoon that something happened.

I felt genuinely sorry for him when he rang my bell and cried, 'My gnomes have disappeared. My lovely gnomes.' But of course, I professed astonishment and ignorance. The police, smiling somewhat, arrived next, questioned us all, but got nowhere at all. And there the matter rested for fifteen years, until last year.

Much has happened since I removed the gnomes. Our youngsters have left home, leaving the house too big for us, so we made a 'granny flat' in it for us to live I. We let the rest of the house to a nice young couple, Simon and Penny. Poor old Hugh, who never replaced his gnomes, and his wife, have moved on to a higher place, and their family have sold the house. And so on, with changes all around.

I said the matter rested until last year. This was the year of the great drought, when water levels all over the country, in rivers, lakes and reservoirs, were falling to dangerous levels.

That was when four mysterious black bags, huddled together, were revealed resting on the bottom of our reservoir. The story soon got around. Apparently, the police thought at first that the bags contained bodies, the result of mass murder, but when they got them up, of course, they were disappointed. Nothing more exciting than twenty garden gnomes seeing the light of day for the first time in fifteen years, and they, incidentally, were in remarkably good condition.

Strangely, they didn't seem to link them with the case of the long missing pets. Or if they did, they must have found out that Hugh and his wife were dead anyway, and the matter was not worth pursuing. So all went quiet again for many months and I said to Sue, 'You won't have to visit me in prison after all.'

But things do come back to haunt you. They have to me, anyway. Those twenty garden gnomes. They're in the garden at the back of my house and I see them every morning when I shave. Sue says with glee, 'It serves you right and I am really glad.' You see, when we let the rest of the house to Simon and Penny, that included the garden as well.

How was I to know that Simon was a gnome-fancier and would buy the lot at a sale of unclaimed recovered stolen goods at the police station the other day? Still, perhaps they'll go away for a weekend soon.

George Yorke

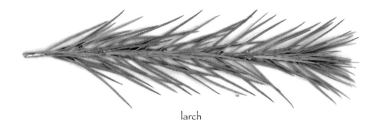

larch

For twenty-five years, George wrote short stories and articles as a hobby. Many of them were published nationally, and a number broadcast by the BBC. With a number of friends, he helped to form the Dean Writers' Circle in 1978, and he acted as its secretary from its inception until shortly before his death in 1998.

CREDITS

Editing by Toni Wilde and John Stanley.

Design, layout and text reworking by the editors.

Illustrations:

Original artwork, pages 6,87,108	John Stanley
Original artwork, pages 23,28,75,116,144	Toni Wilde
Original artwork, page 57	Julian Horsfield
Collage, page 41	Coral Hayward
Collage, page 16	C Hayward/Toni Wilde
Reworked art, pages 34,97	Toni Wilde
Shamrock, page115	David Warren
Photograph, page 62	Ruth Elsdale
Photograph, page 68	Graham Wilde
Photograph, page 80	Anthony Reeve
Photographs, pages 73, 103	Toni Wilde
Photograph, page 125	Natalie Williams
Photographs, pages 5,156	David Cheshire

www.davidcheshirephotography.com

Original leaf inserts sourced in the Forest of Dean, identified, scanned and photographed by the editors.

IT Consultancy   Martyn Field

Cover Design by the editors.
Front Cover – Photograph by Anthony Reeve.
Back Cover – Leaf scans and arrangements by the editors.

189